THE

Solheim Cup

Published by:

PING

PING Inc.
2201 W. Desert Cove
Phoenix, AZ 85029
www.solheimcup.com

Editor - Bob Cantin

THE
Solheim Cup

Library of Congress Control Number: 2005924366

This book is dedicated to the memory of Karsten Solheim.
Women's golf has had no greater angel.

ACKNOWLEDGEMENTS

It has been a privilege and a pleasure to work with so many talented people in the creation, compilation and completion of this book. During the past 26 years in the golf industry, I have been fortunate to meet and become friends with the writers, photographers, graphic artists, designers, sponsors and resource people who have helped make this publication become a reality.

First and foremost, I would like to personally thank Mrs. Karsten (Louise) Solheim and John A. Solheim for their support in approving and helping fund this project. Their encouragement has been uplifting from the start. Their writing of the prologue and epilogue gives keen insight into their innermost feelings about The Solheim Cup.

We are indebted to Ty Votaw, commissioner of the Ladies Professional Golf Association, and to Ian Randell, former chief executive of the Ladies European Tour, for contributing to the financial success of this commemorative volume. From the outset, they recognized the need for it to become a reality and gave it their unqualified backing.

We also wish to thank the following companies, golf clubs and associations and their representatives who willingly committed monetary support to a "sight unseen" publication, having faith that the end result would be a quality read: Waterford Crystal (Mel Morgan); The Golf Channel (David Manougian); The Greenbrier (Steve Baldwin); Winn Grips (Ben Huang); Swedish Golf Federation (Per Adler and Mats Enquist); Tournaments for Charity (Kip Eriksen); Haas-Jordan Umbrellas by Westcott (Thomas Waltz); Golf Pride Grips (Bob Cresante); Aldila (Mike Rossi); Liz Claiborne (Leah Caruso); Rolex (Peter Nicholson); True Temper (David Hallford); Loch Lomond Golf Club (Lyle Anderson and Phil Edlund); Barsebäck Golf & Country Club (Jerry Carlsson and Ulf Öhrvik); Bryan Cave LLP (Troy Froderman); Peter Scott Ltd. (Nick Bannerman); The Martin Agency (Paul McKee); The Cavanagh Law Firm (Dave Van Engelhoven); Perry Ellis Co. (Jim Scully); Halmstad Golfklubb (Mats Malmberg); City of Halmstad (Stig-Ove Rick); NCR Corporation (Bill Saylor); Microsoft Corporation (Ryan Kubacki); and Rich Harvest Farms (Jerry Rich and Holly Alcala).

And to the tremendously talented journalists who made this book come to life, you recounted your experiences while covering Solheim Cup golf with insight and passion. As an editor, I am very fortunate and proud to have assembled such an outstanding team of writers. You are truly among the crème de la crème of the golf writing fraternity, and I look forward to seeing each of you at future Solheim Cups.

Special thanks to our friends and associates David Cannon, Rick Sharp, Kay Bagwell, Stephen Munday, Scott Halleran, Craig Jones, Stuart Franklin, Warren Little, Stephen Szurlej, Bill Wynne, Jerry Wisler, James Quantz Jr., Dale Kirk, Tom Able Green, Jack Stohlman, Holly Alcala, Jerry Rich, Pete Samuels and Rob Griffin for being at the right place at the right time to capture the photographs. Many of your pictures say much more than a thousand words.

Each of the following people know how they helped too. Their guidance, assistance and contributions are greatly appreciated: Cal Brown (former Golf Digest writer and editor); James A. Searle Jr. and Lynn Swann (The Greenbrier); Chris Higgs, Kelly Hyne, Connie Wilson and Carol Kilian (LPGA); Martin Park (LET); Julie DiMarco (Golf World magazine); Jason Keller and Ann Reineking (The Kohler Company); Devin Howell (PGA of America); Brad Carlson, Jennifer De Leonardis and Rick Bond (Sport Graphics); and Peg Adams and Donna Cunning (PING).

And to my wife Marsha, the love and inspiration of my life, your faithful and unlimited behind-the-scenes assistance at each Solheim Cup has been appreciated more than you will ever know, every step of the way.

BOB CANTIN
Editor

TABLE OF CONTENTS

PROLOGUE

MRS. KARSTEN (LOUISE) SOLHEIM
Chairman Emeritus
Karsten Manufacturing Corporation

★ ★ ★

A Ryder Cup style tournament for the top lady golf professionals on either side of the Atlantic? What a wonderful idea! And they, Bill Blue, Commissioner for the Ladies Professional Golf Association at the time and Gregg Shimanski, LPGA vice president of business affairs, were asking my husband Karsten and me if we would be interested in being the founding sponsor of the event?

It was not an unearned opportunity. Karsten Manufacturing Corporation was currently (1990) sponsoring or helping to sponsor four regionally different LPGA golf tournaments: PING-Cellular One Golf Championship (Portland, Oregon), Boston Five Classic (Danvers, Massachusetts), Circle K LPGA Tucson Open (Tucson, Arizona), and the Standard Register Turquoise Classic on our company-owned Moon Valley Country Club course in Phoenix, Arizona. Besides those endeavors, approximately 50 or more of the lady professional golfers were using PING golf equipment and participating in our KMC "thank you for using PING" Pot - a purse to reward PING women golf professionals according to a scale of tournaments played, number of PING clubs used (12 were required with one of the 12 being a PING putter), tournament cuts made and finishing place in the field.

Nevertheless, I had been apprehensive going to the lunch meeting on January 26 in Orlando, FL. For nearly three years Karsten Manufacturing's very popular PING EYE2 irons had been under scrutiny by the United States Golf Association as to whether their U-shaped grooves conformed to the 1984 USGA Rule Book specifications which for the first time permitted square or U-shaped grooves. V-shaped grooves were difficult to cast as opposed to forged clubheads and many, if not most, of the golf equipment manufacturers were switching to the lost wax method of casting iron heads after Karsten Manufacturing had so successfully led the way.

Because of this controversy, in 1989 KMC had done the unthinkable...sued the USGA and shortly after that, also sued the PGA Tour which was threatening to ban the PING EYE2s from men's tournament play. My husband Karsten could think of nothing else at that time, but protecting the hundreds of thousands of happy golfers who were playing PING EYE2 irons. Even at that moment in 1990, son John was in San Diego where the USGA was holding its annual meeting, conferring with outgoing President Bill Battle and others, looking for a solution to the costly dispute.

All of these thoughts were whirling about in my mind as I approached the luncheon site. Was the LPGA Commissioner going to tell us now that the lady tour professionals were going to ban PING EYE2 irons? Already we had lost men players like Fred Couples, Davis Love III, Bob Tway and others. Karsten was approaching 80 years of age. How much more could he take?

So there we were...breathing a sigh of relief when the question was posed by Commissioner Blue. This was not about the grooves at all, but about something that could have true significance to women's golf. We could see that their questions needed a response as soon as possible because the date that was chosen for this new event was November 1990...only 10 months away.

★ ★ ★

Karsten and I knew exactly what they were talking about. We had attended our first Ryder Cup match in Houston in 1967 and almost every one of the biennial events since. We knew nothing about the organization of such an event, but found out that the Ladies Professional Golf Association along with the Women Professional Golfers' European Tour had pretty much laid out the plans...venue (Lake Nona Golf Club near Orlando, Florida), the date, format, etc. All they needed from us at that time was confirmation that we would be the founding sponsor.

It was during phone conversations in mid-March at the Standard Register Turquoise Classic when we put forth the suggestion that we would sponsor the first 10 venues if the event would be named the Karsten Cup. That offer went back to the LPGA to vote on. They came back with the remark that Karsten Cup was too commercial, but they could accept Solheim Cup and so it was agreed.

On June 7th, Karsten and I met with Bill Blue at the Delta Airlines Crown Room at Sky Harbor International Airport in Phoenix to sign the initial papers, but there was much to be decided on the tournament and player criteria. In August of 1990 all parties from both tours met at Wykagyl Country Club in New Rochelle, NY, during the JAL Big Apple Classic to review these important aspects of the matches. (The LPGA was also celebrating its 40th anniversary with a gala dinner at the Waldorf Astoria ballroom.) Then, finally on September 19, the final papers were signed and planning earnestly began for this elite event.

Of course, our responsibility as sponsors did not end with dotting the i's and crossing the t's of a contract; we were the third leg of a triumvirate-the Ladies Professional Golf Association of the United States, the Women Professional Golfers' European Tour and Karsten Manufacturing Corporation, makers of PING Golf Equipment. We all shared a common desire to stage a biennial event that would place women's golf before the eyes of the world and open the doors for young girls and women everywhere to participate in this wonderful game.

Another decision we made as a company and family regarding our sponsorship for the whole tournament was to be completely unbiased and root for both teams regardless of the outcome. We felt that because of Karsten's Norwegian heritage and our corporate interests worldwide, we definitely were an international company.

We at KMC had early on brought our Director of Communications, Robert (Bob) Cantin, forward to act as Project Director for our participation. Bob is the most organized person I know, with his widespread acquaintances in the media, his attention to detail and his innate ability to think through solutions to last minute mix-ups. Bob, with his executive assistant, Peg Adams, kept things to at least appear to be running smoothly.

One important aspect of PING's sponsorship was a decision Karsten and I made right at the start...PING would be a background player. The formidable abilities of these talented lady professional golfers and the countries they represented would take center stage. The fact that PING was there to showcase the event was to be minimized. We would feature great golf amid patriotic pomp and circumstance. Joe Flanagan, WPGET executive director said, "There was a lot of national and international pride at stake." And the inaugural event set the tone for future Solheim Cups.

Some things appeared to take care of themselves. Right away Kevin Hall, Export Sales Manager for Waterford Crystal, came forward with a beautiful crystal trophy. The delicate intricacy of the exquisite cut crystal urn seemed to lend itself to the femininity of a woman's sport. It is a much coveted trophy by both tours.

The LPGA had selected Kathy Whitworth to be captain of the American team and the European Tour had chosen Mickey Walker to lead their team. Both these women, with their outstanding array of personal victories on their respective golf circuits, were unquestioned leaders in their fields. Kathy with her 88 victories may never be equalled by either gender of golfers. Mickey was an outstanding amateur, winning seven tournaments and participating on Curtis Cup and World Cup teams. She also had six professional wins to her credit.

It had been decided that the first venue would have eight players on each side. The Opening Ceremony was held on Thursday of tournament week complete with flag raising and national anthems followed by player introductions by the respective captains. Play would go over three days...Friday, Saturday and Sunday...with team play over the first two days and singles matches taking place on Sunday.

The field would be chosen from earned Solheim Cup points for regular tour play over a two year period. The U.S. Team would have one captain's pick player not necessarily from the earned point list. The European Team would have two captain's picks, four players from the European Tour money list and two European players currently playing on the LPGA Tour. In essence this gave the Europeans four captain's picks. The consensus was, however, that despite the discrepancy between team selection methods, it was a sensible solution for a more competitive tournament. The field was increased to 10 on each side in 1992 and to 12 in 1994 with an alternate added in 1996 and later dropped. Currently the LPGA, whose 12 players must all be born in the USA, has two captain's picks. The LET has the same number of players and five captain's picks. This format has worked very well.

Did we know at the time what this event would mean to women's golf throughout the world? No, we did not. The Ryder Cup had taken about 50 years to gain some of the stature it now enjoys. We hoped it wouldn't take that long. In the beginning people in the golf community felt that the Americans would walk away with the match and were afraid it would not be a very good competition. That first event at Lake Nona proved everyone wrong...the Europeans were, indeed, competitive and out to prove it! Even though the Americans came away with the initial win, the stage was set for exciting rivalry in future Solheim Cups.

At this writing eight Solheim Cups have taken place, each more exciting than the ones before it. The Solheim Cup is spoken of in the media as the most prestigious event on the calendar of the ladies professional golf tours worldwide. The Solheim Family feels honored to have helped promote friendship through golf on both sides of the Atlantic Ocean. Karsten Solheim would be proud, as are his sons, John, Allan and Karsten Louis, who carry on his dream of worldwide friendship through golf.

FOREWORD

KAREN LUNN
Chairman
Board of Directors
Ladies European Tour

On behalf of the staff and members of the Ladies European Tour, I would like to welcome you to this superb commemorative coffee table book which documents the rich and storied history of The Solheim Cup, an event which has developed into the most anticipated spectacle in women's golf every two years.

Since its inception in 1990, The Solheim Cup has provided the attending galleries and millions of television viewers around the globe a veritable feast of patriotism, passion, sportsmanship and golf of the highest quality played by the finest athletes on either side of the Atlantic.

In this unique book, we have commissioned the most esteemed authors and photographers from the golf industry who have illustrated The Solheim Cup from its inauguration to the present day. I am sure you will relish studying each and every article and picture which bring back some fabulous memories and once again raise the heart rate and adrenaline to the level which we all experienced during each event.

Those who have witnessed The Solheim Cup have experienced the full gamut of emotions from start to finish, not only out on the course but on the first tee where the wonderfully competitive but jovial atmosphere is incomparable to anything else in golf.

Photo: David Cannon

One can only imagine the effect that the Cup has on those competing in the cauldron of the golf course in front of partisan yet appreciative galleries amounting to tens of thousands, who over the years have at times braved inclement weather to witness first hand the spectacular events which unfolded in front of them.

Each contest has ebbed and flowed tantalizingly and like every matchplay competition, there are those unforgettable moments which stand out. Many will never forget Carin Koch holing the winning putt on the 17th green at Loch Lomond in 2000 in virtual darkness, and the match played in 2003 between Suzann Pettersen and Annika Sörenstam for Europe against two of the USA's finest players, Kelly Robbins and Laura Diaz.

That match will be remembered as one of the finest four-ball matches ever recorded in matchplay golf. It was truly stunning to watch with all four players firing birdie after birdie in a nail biting thriller. When Suzann holed the curling ten-footer on the 18th green to win a match which no team deserved to lose, supporters from both teams and the world's media conceded it was arguably the finest display of matchplay golf in recent history.

The match was the catalyst for Europe to go on and win the event in Sweden, a country which has been heralded as the home of women's golf and where, in 2007, The Solheim Cup will again be played. It was also a fitting tribute to the Solheim family that a Norwegian player holed the putt which secured Europe's victory in the first-ever and biggest Solheim Cup staged in Scandinavia.

The event in Sweden highlighted the phenomenal growth over 14 years of The Solheim Cup, establishing it as one of the most prestigious events on the sporting calendar and raising the bar to a new level for women's golf.

From its early beginnings at Lake Nona Golf Club in Florida, the event has grown in stature year upon year and in Sweden we welcomed nearly 500 journalists, photographers, radio broadcasters and television reporters to the event, which helped put women's golf in the prime position of the world's newspapers and in millions of television homes around the globe.

The reason for this is simple. Karsten Solheim had a dream and, thanks to his foresight and commitment, it has become a reality. The Solheim Cup embodies perfectly the origins of not only the game of golf, but sport itself. One team against another, playing for pride, passion, united under one banner and without remuneration in any way, shape or form.

Golf is in essence a singular game, and when an event can bring two disparate groups of single minded people together as a unit for a week, it changes the way people think about each other.

The mutual respect, camaraderie, integrity and passion shown by each team at The Solheim Cup is a credit to these golfing gladiators. From a European perspective, the unity and cooperation shown by our teams over the years, who hail from different countries, speak different languages and enjoy diverse cultures, is one that the politicians across the European Union nations can only but dream of.

The Ladies European Tour offers its heartfelt thanks to the Solheim Family for their ongoing commitment to women's professional golf which has allowed us to bring Karsten's original concept to a level for which we can all take great pride.

FOREWORD

TY M. VOTAW
Commissioner
Ladies Professional Golf
Association

Since I began my tenure with the LPGA in 1991, I have had the privilege of attending seven Solheim Cups, and I consider each and every one a new highlight in my career. I have, with the rest of the world, watched as the competition has blossomed into one of the greatest sporting events women's golf has ever seen. Each time, I expect to be thrilled and mesmerized by the talent, patriotism and heart displayed by the world's best golfers, and I have never been disappointed.

There is truly no greater honor than representing your country or continent in your chosen sport. Earning the right to compete in The Solheim Cup is an honor and a privilege unmatched by any accolade the golfing community can bestow upon a player. That is what makes the event so unforgettable to the athletes and so special to the fans.

For more than a decade, The Solheim Cup and the players who have donned red, white and blue or blue and gold have honored the ideals and values that were the centerpiece of this event when it was created by Karsten and Louise Solheim in 1990. Those ideals and values are an ongoing commitment to honor and duty, not only to country or continent, but also to teammates, and, perhaps more importantly, to fellow competitors; an appreciation of and respect for the integrity of both the individual and the competition; and finally, an abiding and deep-rooted emphasis on sportsmanship and fair dealing in all they do.

The Solheim Cup has become a shining example of purity in sport due to the willingness of each player to uphold those values and to commit herself to playing for the love of the game. And in a day of words like 'salary caps,' 'work stoppages,' and behavioral problems of professional athletes dominating the sports pages, how inspiring it has been to witness The Solheim Cup, a beautiful illustration of all that is right in the world of sports.

The players compete in The Solheim Cup for pride and for their countries or continents. There is never a question of whether they want to play, never a doubt about the importance of the competition, never a thought given to if it will benefit them financially. I have said before that The Solheim Cup is perhaps one of the last shining examples of purity in sport, and what a tremendous example to our children and to the world.

I know you will enjoy this first-ever Solheim Cup coffee table book. For many of you, it will be a trip down memory lane, as it was for me. I still get goose bumps reading about the incredible moments in Solheim Cup history, and this remarkable collection of stories and photos certainly paints a vivid picture of what I feel very fortunate to have witnessed first hand. And for those of you perhaps discovering The Solheim Cup for the first time, I trust the excitement relayed within these pages will make you a fan of this unique competition for many years to come.

Photo: Courtesy of Lake Nona Golf C

1990

Lake Nona Golf Club

The perfect place to launch a legacy

BY TIM ROSAFORTE

Photo: Courtesy of Lake Nona Golf Club

At precisely 10:10 a.m. on November 16, 1990, 39-year-old Pat Bradley hit the first tee shot of The Solheim Cup.

"TO MAKE HISTORY AND START HISTORY.
THAT'S AN HONOR." Pat Bradley

★ ★ ★

In the European team room they were referred to as "God and God," but Pat Bradley and Nancy Lopez didn't feel deserving of reverential treatment. "We were petrified," Lopez said. Standing with them on the tee that day at Lake Nona GC in Orlando were Laura Davies and Alison Nicholas of Great Britain. It was Friday, Nov. 16, 1990, a steamy fall morning in Central Florida. For six minutes they waited until the clock tower signified it was time to play away, the nervousness building by the second. "Heck," said the always pensive Bradley, "it's like waiting for the Space Shuttle to go."

★ ★ ★

The Ladies European Tour's executive director, Joe Flanagan, worked behind the scenes for two years to help bring The Solheim Cup to fruition.

Bradley could see the launch the previous night from the clubhouse, where the United States team anxiously awaited the first day in Solheim Cup history. It would be a day to be long remembered by Karsten Solheim, the founder of this international competition between the LPGA and the Women Professional Golfer's European Tour. And if what Solheim and his family created represented one small step for Bradley and her teammates, it was one giant step for women's golf worldwide. "I feel like a pioneer," said Kathy Whitworth, captain of the United States team.

At the same time, Whitworth was cautious. America had not won a Ryder Cup since 1983, so she delivered her "Knute Rockne speech" to the team on Thursday night before the competition, making sure they didn't take the Europeans lightly. "The Ryder Cup should be a lesson for us all," Whitworth said. "You don't take the cream of the crop and not expect them to be ready."

Mickey Walker, the European captain, fed off the inspired Ryder Cup triumphs of Europe in 1985, 1987, and the draw in 1989, trying to instill in her team the same defiance that Tony Jacklin brought to his team. "We're the best players in Europe," Walker said. "Why should we be intimidated?"

"Dressed to the nines," the USA ninesome posed for a photo call.

Helen Alfredsson has a "nail-biting" experience in handling her country's colors.

On that note, Bradley and Lopez went down in the first match of the opening day, proving the fears of Whitworth and that "God and God" were human after all. The same couldn't be said for the rest of the United States team, which swept the three remaining matches without making a bogey or losing a hole. It was a precursor of the eventual rout administered by the American team that featured three other mega-stars in Betsy King, Beth Daniel and Patty Sheehan. The U.S. side had decided advantages in major championships (14 to 2), total victories (151 to 71) and what Whitworth felt was the biggest advantage, pro experience (10.7 years to 5.4).

Whitworth could have pulled a Ben Hogan, simply introduced her team as "the eight best players in the world," and left it at that. Other than Davies, Liselotte Neumann and Helen Alfredsson, this was predominantly a developmental team. "There might come a point when the Europeans will be competitive in this format," said Bradley. "But it won't be for a while. Not with [players like] Lopez, Bradley, King, Daniel and Sheehan in their prime."

"YOU DON'T TAKE THE CREAM OF THE CROP AND NOT EXPECT THEM TO BE READY." Kathy Whitworth

The Tom Fazio-designed Lake Nona Golf Club provided a scenic and challenging venue for the inaugural Solheim Cup.

"I KNOW WE HAD THE BEST PLAYERS IN THE WORLD AND WE WANTED TO SHOW IT," SAID KING. "SIXTEEN-NOTHING WAS MY GOAL."

Betsy King

Photo: Stephen Munday

Betsy King's 2nd shot was headed for Lake Nona but caromed off a tall tree onto the 18th green, permitting her to par the hole and halve the match with Pam Wright.

Photo: David Cannon

So it was not about the score in this one as much as the ground breaking. For record keeping it was $11^1/_2$ to $4^1/_2$ but in the cold light of history there was no disgrace in losing by seven points to this juggernaut of LPGA Hall of Famers. Especially with the American team fired up to defend the honor of its golfing nation. There was talk that U.S. Ryder Cup captain Dave Stockton might want to import the attitude adopted by Whitworth's players, Bradley and King in particular. "I know we had the best players in the world and we wanted to show it," said King. "Sixteen-nothing was my goal."

The early upset of Bradley and Lopez spoiled the shutout, but not the ultimate waxing. The United States led 3-1 after the first day of foursomes and 6-2 after the second day of four-balls. The key for Whitworth was getting by the first day in a game they weren't accustomed to playing. "I'm not so confident that I'm overconfident," said Daniel. "But we're in good shape. Alternate shots are a real tough format for us. They grow up playing it as kids. We never play it. However, I think Kathy Whitworth did an excellent job teaming us up."

Only one match went to the difficult 18th hole, but the Florida sun majestically settled there every afternoon.

"I HAVEN'T SEEN THE 16TH HOLE HERE," SAID DANIEL. "AND TOMORROW I HOPE I DON'T SEE THE 12TH."

Beth Daniel

USA Captain Kathy Whitworth adds another trophy to her record of 88 victories on the LPGA Tour.

It didn't matter who Whitworth paired together; it seemed to work. In Cathy Gerring and Dottie Pepper, she had her two youngest and demonstrative players. In Bradley and Lopez, she had her legends. In Patty Sheehan and Rosie Jones she mixed fire with fire. In King and Daniel, she had two former Furman University teammates who were the LPGA's last two respective Players of the Year. "Betsy and I know each other's games so well that I can tell you what she's hitting without looking in her bag," said Daniel. "I know because she's hitting the same thing I'm hitting."

King and Daniel played the best team golf for the Americans, posting victories of 5 and 4 against Trish Johnson of England and Marie-Laure de Lorenzi of France on Friday and 4 and 3 against Davies-Nicholas on Saturday. In their Day Two match, Daniel and King birdied five out of six holes to close out Europe's toughest side on the 16th. Whitworth's second-best team turned out to be Sheehan and Rosie Jones. They were -4 when the match ended with a birdie on the 13th hole the first day, and earned a tough point in the four-balls against Johnson, the best player on the WPGET that year, and de Lorenzi.

Solheim Cup match founders Karsten and Louise Solheim beam their approval during Opening Ceremonies.

Photo: David Cannon

Walker, who played the LPGA Tour in the seventies, went more with style of play. Her chance to get back in the competition rode on the play of Davies, who said before the matches she was "prepared to wager anyone that we will win." Struggling to hit fairways on Saturday, she put Nicholas in uncompromising positions and they were no match for the 10 birdies thrown at them by Daniel and King. Europe's only victory that day was posted by Neumann and Pam Wright against the Doublemint Twins, Gerring and Pepper.

Knowing she needed to win six of the eight remaining singles matches, and gain a halve in the seventh, European captain Mickey Walker looked at the Sunday singles lineups and said quite frankly, "We're going to have to play our boots off." The Americans were not going to let up. "I haven't seen the 16th hole here," said Daniel. "And tomorrow I hope I don't see the 12th."

Photo: David Cannon

Cathy Gerring won two matches in her only Solheim Cup appearance, her career cut short after sustaining burns on her hands and face during a fire incident on tour.

Photo: David Cannon

Winner of the US Women's Open two years prior, Sweden's Lisolette Neumann scored 7 birdies in one round at Lake Nona.

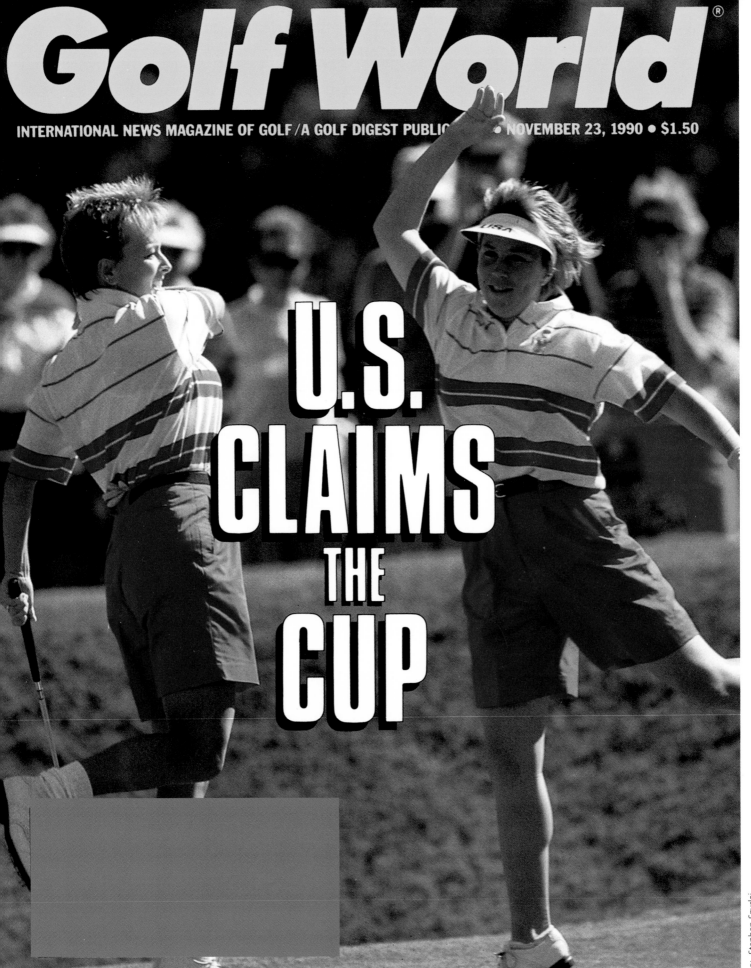

Golf World ®

INTERNATIONAL NEWS MAGAZINE OF GOLF/A GOLF DIGEST PUBLIC ● NOVEMBER 23, 1990 ● $1.50

U.S. CLAIMS THE CUP

High fives were flying as Dottie (Pepper) Mochrie and Cathy Gerring won their first day foursomes match 6 & 5 over Pam Wright and Liselotte Neumann. It was the event's first golf magazine cover.

32   The Solheim Cup

Beth Daniel won all of her matches at Lake Nona, the only player on either team to accomplish this feat.

The going was tough for Trish Johnson as she sustained the worst defeat in Solheim Cup history, losing to Pat Bradley 8 & 7.

Only one match reached the 18th all week, and ironically it was King who reached it for the Americans. At that point, the outcome had long been decided in a series of lopsided singles victories, none more convincing than Bradley's 8 and 7 crushing of Trish Johnson. Bradley started with birdies on seven of her first 11 holes, denying Johnson an opportunity to get rhythm. "She really didn't have room to breathe," said Bradley. "Even my pace walking down the fairway left her in the dust."

Lopez earned the winning point against Nicholas, who spoke about the golf instruction book she received for her 19th birthday, written by her idol and opponent. The victory meant a great deal to Lopez, who was Whitworth's captain's pick. "There was a rumor I wouldn't accept if Kathy chose me, and I don't know how that got started," she said. "I had my fingers crossed I'd be asked to play." Whitworth proved to be a perfect captain, saying quite simply, "I just hope I didn't get in the players way too much." But she was hands-on when she needed to be. On Friday, for example, she drove up to the sixth hole in a cart and consulted with King, who was leaning toward hitting an 8-iron into the 145-yard par-3. Knowing players had trouble with the yardage, and had been coming up short, she passed on the information to King, who hit "a little 7" to 2 inches. "We may be a team of individuals," said Daniel, "but we all love playing for Whit."

KNOWING SHE NEEDED TO WIN SIX OF THE EIGHT REMAINING SINGLES MATCHES, AND GAIN A HALVE IN THE SEVENTH, EUROPEAN CAPTAIN MICKEY WALKER LOOKED AT THE SUNDAY SINGLES LINEUPS AND SAID QUITE FRANKLY, "WE'RE GOING TO HAVE TO PLAY OUR BOOTS OFF."

USA		EUROPE	
Kathy Whitworth, Captain	Texas	Mickey Walker, Captain	England
Pat Bradley	Massachusetts	Helen Alfredsson	Sweden
Beth Daniel	South Carolina	Laura Davies	England
Cathy Gerring	Indiana	Marie-Laure de Lorenzi	France
Rosie Jones	California	Trish Johnson	England
Betsy King	Pennsylvania	Liselotte Neumann	Sweden
Nancy Lopez	California	Alison Nicholas	England
Dottie (Pepper) Mochrie	New York	Dale Reid	Scotland
Patty Sheehan	Vermont	Pam Wright	Scotland

In the end the Europeans said they weren't outplayed, but merely outputted. "We felt it was an unjust result because we were right up there with them in the fairway and inside them on the greens," said Davies. "We just didn't make any putts." Walker concurred, to an extent. "I don't think we could have beaten them, but the results would have been closer," she said. "The difference has been on the greens, really. We should be proud of ourselves. We learned a lot and we went down fighting."

The Europeans should have been proud. The collection of talent playing for Whitworth was arguably the strongest nucleus of golfers in American history. The Big Five of Lopez, Bradley, King, Sheehan and Daniel were all close to the pinnacle of their respective careers. Europe, as Davies said, was a young team that could only get better. With Annika Sorenstam still four years away from her first Solheim Cup, this was part of a learning experience. "I felt bad for them," Whitworth said. "It was like they got caught in a buzz saw."

> "THE DIFFERENCE HAS BEEN ON THE GREENS, REALLY. WE SHOULD BE PROUD OF OURSELVES. WE LEARNED A LOT AND WE WENT DOWN FIGHTING."
>
> Mickey Walker, European Team Captain

"I HAD MY FINGERS CROSSED
I'D BE ASKED TO PLAY." Nancy Lopez

Photo: David Cannon

"I'm thrilled, it's a great feeling. It is amazing how important it is to win when you are representing your country," said Nancy Lopez, Captain Whitworth's wild card pick.

Photo: Courtesy of Dalmahoy Hotel Golf & Country Club

1992

Dalmahoy Hotel Golf & Country Club

A tigress off the leash in Scotland

BY PATRICIA DAVIES

Photo: Bill Wynne

The Royal Air Force Aerobatic Team, known as the Red Arrows, performs a colorful fly-by during the Opening Ceremonies.
It is the only 9-plane precision flying squadron operating in the world today.

★ ★ ★

The result of The Solheim Cup at Dalmahoy was a foregone conclusion. It was no contest. It was the sorceresses against the apprentices, women against girls, the mighty mistresses of the United States against the minnows of Europe. The score would be so one-sided that it would diminish the value of the match and leave women's golf floundering in its own little, unconsidered puddle, a backwater far removed from the mainstream of the game. It would be a rout and one big yawn.

★ ★ ★

Well, it was a rout but no one was yawning when the Europeans, inspired by a Laura Davies rampant, marmelised the Americans in the singles on the last day, winning seven and losing only three, to win the match by the astounding margin of $11\frac{1}{2}$ points to $6\frac{1}{2}$. "This has to be one of the sporting achievements of the century," said Mickey Walker, Europe's captain and if she exaggerated, it was not by much. "It's unbelievable. We didn't just beat them. We outplayed them totally. I really believe that when they came over here they thought they would win comfortably. Now I think they're in shock. So am I, for a different reason."

It wasn't just Walker who was euphoric. On an amazing afternoon when the quality of the golf lit up a dull, dreich October day and the cheers of some 8,000 fans were tinged with disbelief, Mark McCormack, once called the "most powerful man in sports" by Sports Illustrated, was so engrossed that he tramped round in the rain without an umbrella or waterproofs, all thoughts of a quick getaway forgotten. Tony Jacklin, who had led Europe to victory in the Ryder Cup in 1985 and 1987 and retained the trophy with a tie in 1989, was so entranced that he stayed glued to Ceefax, a teletext service. Television had shunned covering the event live, deeming it a genteel, lowkey garden party of no general interest, a mismatch that was an invitation to channel hop. It was a monumental misjudgment. The photographs by themselves show that it was a classic contest, full of drama, passion, exhilaration, disappointment and no little skill. It was golf at its best, exciting, enthralling, electrifying and just what the match needed. The Solheim was a tigress off the leash.

Photo: Steve Rose

Little did Catrin Nilsmark know as she holed the winning 2-foot putt that she would captain another European winning Solheim Cup team 11 years later.

Photo: David Cannon

A "sea of blue" on the Sunday leaderboard provides a fitting backdrop for European Captain Mickey Walker, winner of the Waterford Crystal Solheim Cup.

"IT'S AN INCREDIBLE ACHIEVEMENT THAT I DON'T FEEL ANYBODY COULD HAVE POSSIBLY ENVISIONED. TO HAVE BEATEN PEOPLE WHO HAVE ACHIEVED SO MUCH, I'M SPEECHLESS."

European Captain Mickey Walker

European players transport Captain Walker to the victorious Closing Ceremonies.

"THIS IS A HISTORIC DAY. I KNEW WE COULD DO IT, AND WE PROVED WE'VE GOT WHAT IT TAKES TO BE SUCCESSFUL. THESE WOMEN, QUITE SIMPLY, HAVE DONE WHAT THE MEN'S RYDER CUP TEAM FAILED TO DO."

Andrea Doyle, executive director, WPG European Tour

English countrywomen Kitrina Douglas, Laura Davies, Trish Johnson and partially hidden Alison Nicholas enjoy a memorable moment with the Solheim Cup.

Charlie Mechem, the LPGA's affable, astute commissioner, maintained his equilibrium, his perspective and his humour after the upset. "Let's go to press release plan B," he remarked wryly to Elaine Scott, his head of communications. "For me," he said, "the single most important thing was that the quality of the golf was outstanding. Our business is, first of all, women's golf and anything that helps that worldwide can only be good for us." And he had no problem with the uninhibited European celebrations, when even the Scots eschewed their traditional stoicism. "I thought the object of the exercise was to win," he smiled.

Two years after their hammering at Lake Nona, the Europeans were more battle-hardened and much less in awe of their illustrious opponents, who had 147 titles and 21 major championships among them, and the home side's determination to prove themselves was already fierce before they read the words that motivated them to surpass even their own expectations. It was Beth Daniel who lit the blue touchpaper and introduced the bit of needle that was manna from heaven to the tabloids and did all Walker's motivating for her. Daniel, a sublime talent with a combustible streak, was quoted in Golf Digest as saying, "You could put any one of us on the European side and make it better but the only Europeans who could help us are Laura Davies and Liselotte Neumann." It sounded arrogant and Daniel denied ever having said it but the damage was done. The Europeans were furious and Davies loyally said, "It's bloody ridiculous, absolute nonsense, a load of old rubbish."

"ONE OF THE GREATEST SPORTING
ACHIEVEMENTS OF THE CENTURY." Mickey Walker

42 *The Solheim Cup*

The Solheim family joins the winning European team. From left, Mrs. John (Rhonda) Solheim, John Solheim, Karsten Solheim, Mrs. Karsten (Louise) Solheim and Allan Solheim.

> "THIS HAS TO BE ONE OF THE GREATEST SPORTING ACHIEVEMENTS OF THE CENTURY. IT'S INCREDIBLE. I THINK THEY (THE AMERICANS) MUST BE IN SHOCK. I KNOW I AM."
>
> European Captain Mickey Walker.

It was, however, a sustainable argument. Davies and Neumann had both won the US Women's Open and were proven world-class performers, but even though Florence Descampe, a precocious Belgian, had won the McCall's LPGA Classic at Stratton Mountain a few weeks earlier, there was no disputing that on paper the Europeans were not in the same league as opponents like Daniel, Pat Bradley, Betsy King, Juli Inkster, Patty Sheehan, Meg Mallon and Dottie Mochrie (nee and now Pepper), who was undoubtedly the best player in the world at the time. Danielle Ammaccapane, who had won three times, was having the best season of her career and Brandie Burton, just 20, was seen as a superstar in waiting. Deb Richard, the other member of the team, was a solid, consistent player who had won twice the previous year. The bookmakers made them 6-1 on favourites. How could they lose?

By reaping the whirlwind. On the defensive, post Daniel, the Americans, whose captain Kathy Whitworth had flown home when her mother died, were never allowed to settle and Alice Miller, the president elect of the LPGA Tournament Division, who substituted for Whitworth, had a torrid time. "It was a week of adversity," she said. The Europeans hit the fairways running and once on the grass, they did not just tear up the paper of the form book, they shredded it into confetti.

Belgium's long-hitting Florence Descampe made her only Solheim Cup appearance at Dalmahoy.

Euphoria reigns on the 16th green as Catrin Nilsmark sinks the winning putt for Europe.

"I WAS SHAKING, REALLY SHAKING ALL OVER," SHE ADMITTED, "BUT THEN I THOUGHT, 'I CAN MAKE THIS PUTT WITH MY EYES CLOSED.'"

Catrin Nilsmark after holing the winning putt.

Helen Alfredsson (white hat) and Lisolette Neumann (visor) posted 2-0-1 records at Dalmahoy.

> "WE WERE GOING WILD.
> I DON'T THINK ANYBODY
> EXPECTED WHAT WE DID
> TODAY."
>
> Laura Davies after first round play.

High 5's were plentiful in the Davies-Nicholas pairing.

Davies and Alison Nicholas, the Little and Large of foursomes pairings, set the tone. "We've got her," Davies yelled to her diminutive partner on hearing the draw for the foursomes. "We've got King and Daniel." First off, Davies and Nicholas had six birdies in the first ten holes, including four in a row from the 7th, to be four up. They eventually won, nervewrackingly, by one hole in a match that had everything, including a rules rumpus when there was a row over squeegeeing the soggy greens. "Are you going to shut up while I play my shot or what?" Nicholas asked at one stage. These were patently not the shrinking, apologetic violets of Lake Nona. These lambs were ready to do the slaughtering.

In match two, Neumann and Helen Alfredsson, jabbering together in Swedish, were more like rampaging Vikings than the all-American Swedes known to Bradley and Mochrie and won by 2 and 1. Ammaccapane and Mallon always had the edge over Descampe and Trish Johnson in the third match and won at the 18th but it was Europe's day when Dale Reid and Pam Wright, the Scots, halved with Inkster and Sheehan after coming from two down with three to play.

Photo: David Cannon

What a difference a match play day makes, as the Americans enjoy the thrill of victory...

"WE'RE DISAPPOINTED, BUT WE WERE OUTPLAYED. I DON'T FEEL WE PLAYED TO OUR POTENTIAL AS A TEAM AND THE EUROPEANS PLAYED EXTREMELY WELL."

Juli Inkster

Photo: Stephen Munday

...and within 24 hours, suffer the agony of defeat!

The four-balls on day two were just as nerve-shredding. Davies and Nicholas, doing their imitation of the indomitable Ballesteros and Olazabal Ryder Cup duo, held off Inkster and Sheehan by one hole with a better-ball score of 66, six under par, to 67. Burton and Richard halved with Johnson and Descampe; Mallon holed a birdie putt of six feet at the last to stave off Reid and Wright, who had been four down at the turn and Bradley, paired with Mochrie again, hit her second shot at the 18th to two feet, securing a half when both Alfredsson and Neumann missed birdie chances. The Americans, one point behind, celebrated as though they had won the Cup, never anticipating the seismic somersault of the singles.

Davies continued to be the inspiration. In the top singles, she outdrove Burton by 50 yards at the first, 495 yards, uphill, sodden and hit another driver onto the green for the first of seven birdies. They were all square after 11 holes but Davies had an irresistible surge of three birdies in the next four holes and was conceded another birdie at the 16th, where Burton waved her white baseball cap in surrender. Jim Webb, deputy commissioner of the LPGA, commented, "If Laura played with that level of intensity and commitment every week, she'd win six times a year and ten million dollars. "

"I'd be in the loony bin," said Davies.

EUROPE		USA	
Mickey Walker, Captain	England	Kathy Whitworth, Captain	Texas
Helen Alfredsson	Sweden	Danielle Ammaccapane	New York
Laura Davies	England	Pat Bradley	Massachusetts
Florence Descampe	Belgium	Brandie Burton	California
Kitrina Douglas	England	Beth Daniel	South Carolina
Trish Johnson	England	Juli Inkster	California
Liselotte Neumann	Sweden	Betsy King	Pennsylvania
Alison Nicholas	England	Meg Mallon	Massachusetts
Catrin Nilsmark	Sweden	Dottie (Pepper) Mochrie	New York
Dale Reid	Scotland	Deb Richard	Louisiana
Pam Wright	Scotland	Patty Sheehan	Vermont

Alfredsson beat Ammaccapane, Johnson beat Sheehan, the US and British Open champion, and the scoreboards took on a blue hue. Inkster, Daniel and Richard posted some red but the blue tidal wave rolled inexorably on. Wright, no titles, was two down after three to Bradley, 30 titles, including six majors, when she looked at the sea of blue and admitted, "I was damned if I was going to lose. I was playing well and I knew I could beat Pat. I played out of my head."

Towels and tears were the Sunday order of the day as Danielle Ammaccapane lost her singles match to Helen Alfredsson 4 & 3.

And then there was Catrin Nilsmark. Kept on the sidelines until the singles, she played Mallon, the US Open and LPGA champion in 1991 and winner of both her matches thus far. Nilsmark, 25, from Gothenburg, without a victory as a professional, won the first two holes and was never less than two up in a match that ended with scenes of joyous abandon on the 16th green, where the Swede hit a majestic 3-iron to 18 feet, then holed the winning putt from no more than two feet. "I was shaking, really shaking all over," she admitted, "but then I thought, 'I can make this putt with my eyes closed.'" And she did. "It was our moment," Nilsmark said.

England's Trish Johnson won the cheerleading and high jump awards as another European putt dropped in the Saturday four-balls.

"IT WAS OUR MOMENT."

Catrin Nilsmark

Photo: David Cannon

The European caddies had a song for it:

"We're on the march with Mickey's army

We're on the road to Dalmahoy

And we'll really shake them up

When we've won The Solheim Cup

'Cause we're the famous European team."

As one beaming Scotsman noted,

"It disnae scan but it disnae matter."

The Solheim Cup was on the march.

Photo: Courtesy of The Greenbrier

1994

The Greenbrier

America's Resort smiles on the Americans

BY JAIME DIAZ

Photo: David Cannon

Tulips in full bloom against the classic facade of The Greenbrier's north entrance where The Solheim Cup photo call took place.

★ ★ ★

I retain some rich images of the 1994 Solheim Cup. My first look at The Greenbrier Hotel, a giant of Georgian architecture nestled majestically in the West Virginia foothills, immediately and permanently resolved any confusion I might have harbored about the term "grand." And I'll never forget listening to the then 82-year-old Sam Snead hold court on a veranda as I sat scratching the belly of his wonderful golden retriever, Meister. But most of all I think of Beth Daniel on the 18th green.

For all the bucolic grandeur of the setting, the unceasing sensation at The Greenbrier was pressure. Two years before the American women had been trounced at the second Solheim Cup in Dalmahoy, Scotland, an upset that had upended the presumption that the best women's golf was played on the LPGA Tour. At The Greenbrier, the American women were expected to uphold country, tour and individual reputation like never before. To a player, this Solheim Cup meant more than any major championship.

I've been to hyper-charged Ryder Cups, most notably at Kiawah Island in 1991 and Brookline in 1999. But - call me sexist if you will - there is something about the way women athletes process pressure that emits more tension into the atmosphere than do typically more inward-directed male jocks. It may be the inverse of a woman's more empathetic, sensitive and sharing nature - just as they feel our pain more acutely than most men, so do we feel theirs. Women tend to want to make everyone feel OK, and given the pain and embarrassment caused by the result at Dalmahoy, they had a daunting task.

★ ★ ★

SOLHEIM CUP

Laura Davies was enthused when Sam Snead watched her hit practice balls and told her she had good timing.

"ONCE YOU'RE ON THE TEAM, YOU DON'T WANT OFF. I WANT TO GO TO THEIR TURF AND KEEP THE CUP." Tammie Green

Photo: David Cannon

No one seemed more burdened by the pressure than Daniel. In 1994 she led the LPGA money list, won four tournaments, the Vare Trophy for lowest scoring average and Player of the Year honors on her way to a Hall of Fame career.

But at The Greenbrier she looked stricken. Always tightly wound, her thin face seemed more drawn, her long gait quicker, and her elegant swing shorter and more rushed. All week long, she asked her caddie, Greg Sheridan, to bring extra water, "because I had cotton mouth so bad."

A lot of it may have been due to unwittingly making herself The Solheim Cup's lightening rod. A couple of years before, she had made the comment that while any member of the American squad could have played for the opposition and strengthened its team, only two European players, Laura Davies and Liselotte Neumann, could have helped the Americans. It made for bulletin board material in the European locker room, further fueling their nothing-to-lose mission. "I feel sorry for the Americans," said Davies. "If they win, it will be, 'Who the devil did you beat?' If they lose, it will be 'To those bums?'" Loose and inspired, the Europeans were again greater than the sum of their parts, and after the first two days battled to a 5-5 tie, with everything riding on the Sunday singles.

So the then 38-year-old Daniel understandably tossed and turned all night before her singles match with Trish Johnson of England. On the first tee, she seemed to be shivering as much from nerves as the autumn chill. The match was an exhibition in jittery, scratchy golf, with Daniel finally taking a one up lead to the 18th tee. Both players hit the green, but Johnson putted long, and then missed the comebacker. Daniel, with two putts from four feet for the win, looked surprised and then relieved when her putt was conceded. She shook hands with Johnson, and then simply stood still.

The Greenbrier president and managing director Ted J. Kleisner played host to the 1994 Solheim Cup.

"THIS WAS A MAJESTIC TRIUMPH FOR WOMEN'S GOLF. TRULY, WHAT WE SAW (AT THE GREENBRIER) WAS HISTORY IN THE MAKING."

Terry Coates, executive director, WPG European Tour.

LPGA Commissioner Charles S. Mechem Jr. hailed the 1994 Solheim Cup as a "watershed event" in the history of the LPGA.

First her caddie hugged her. Then her father, Bob, came out on the green and applied a longer embrace. When Daniel finally turned to a reporter, she could only shake her head as the words refused to come.

"Oh man," she finally said. "Oh man."

After pursing her lips, she managed, "I'm sorry. It just means so much." It's at such moments it becomes clear that no matter how aloof and expressionless most professionals appear during tournament competition, there is a powerful reservoir of passion and emotion under the surface. That in fact the primary challenge is to keep those emotions at bay so that they don't ruin the physical ability to perform. How this powerful force is channeled is the key to success in big events. Turning pressure into performance at The Greenbrier was the intuitive alchemy of U.S. team captain, JoAnne Carner.

The then 55-year-old Carner remains the greatest amateur woman match player of modern times, undefeated in Curtis Cup singles with a 91 percent winning percentage in USGA match play competitions. But more than her record, what made Carner a leader was her bigger than life presence, natural warmth and innate empathy. With her slow growl of a chain smoker's voice and languid, world weary manner, it was endearing rather than grating when she donned a garish "USA" baseball cap covered in red, white and blue sequins. Never one to show a trace of anxiety - her metabolism is so naturally relaxed she routinely drank four cups of coffee before competitive rounds just to get herself going - Carner was the perfect counterbalance to her nervous charges, a nurturing and protective mother bear inspiring security and confidence.

Brilliant fall colors added to the pristine condition of The Greenbrier Course.

"THIS IS GREAT FOR WOMEN'S GOLF. TOO MUCH HAS BEEN MADE ABOUT WHO WINS AND WHO LOSES, ABOUT WHO'S BETTER AND WHO'S NOT BETTER. IT DOESN'T MAKE ANY DIFFERENCE. WOMEN'S GOLF WON HERE, WHICH WAS GOOD BECAUSE WE HAVE A LOT OF CATCHING UP TO DO. WE CERTAINLY DON'T NEED TO BE FIGHTING EACH OTHER." Beth Daniel

Autumn at The Greenbrier makes for a nice pairing of Alison Nicholas and maple leaves.

Photo: David Cannon

"PEOPLE WHO WATCHED THIS TOURNAMENT SAW SOME OF THE GREATEST GOLF SHOTS, UNDER PRESSURE, THAT THEY'LL EVER SEE — BY A MAN OR A WOMAN." Beth Daniel

Singing at The Solheim Cup's 1st tee originated at The Greenbrier, as this European-dominated gallery can attest.

Photo: David Cannon

Photo: David Cannon

Michelle McGann served as an "alternate" in 1994 but made the team outright in 1996–her only two Solheim Cup appearances.

"I forced them to think of only winning the first hole," she explained. "I said, 'I don't want to hear anything else. I want you to stand on that first tee and I want you to win the first hole for me. If you are thinking you are going to win it, you are thinking much more aggressively.' I squelched all of that negative stuff. I told them if they were nervous I would get them some Vaseline for their teeth to quiet the chattering."

Meanwhile, the press had no such concerns, and in the off hours lived like the swells at The Greenbrier media rate. There were horse drawn carriage rides, skeet shooting, bowling, dinners with white glove service. Just standing in front of the hotel's White House-like facade, or walking around the two-century-old place's 6500 acres - all of it bursting with a full autumnal explosion of red and gold - let us feel like self-satisfied robber barons from the Gilded Age. The old world icon also had acquired some modern intrigue. At the time of The Solheim Cup, it had just been revealed that during the Eisenhower years, a gigantic concrete bunker, built with the intention of being a refuge for Congress in the event of a nuclear attack, had been secretly constructed below one of the newer wings of the hotel. Reaching as deep as 700 feet underground, the 112,000 square foot complex contained a 400 seat cafeteria and 18 dormitories sleeping 60 people each. More than one U.S. player thought the bunker might be a good place to lay low in the event Europe won again. That fear, despite Big Momma's best efforts, made the actual competition a tense affair, with several American stars showing that their scar tissue from Dalmahoy was far from healed.

"You wouldn't think that the great veteran I'm supposed to be would have been the nervous wreck out there, but I was," said Patty Sheehan, admitting that Solheim Cup rookie Sherri Steinhauer had carried her in their alternate shot match against Pam Wright and Johnson. Nerves also befell the American's two other future Hall of Famers, Betsy King and Daniel.

The U.S. was in desperate need of veteran leadership, and it came in the intense visage of Dottie Mochrie. Having played poorly at Dalmahoy herself, the then 29-year-old winner of eight LPGA events came to The Greenbrier in emotional overdrive. To the game face what Mickey Wright is to the golf swing, Mochrie dyed her hair red two weeks before the event, and played every match inflamed.

She went over the line in the Saturday better ball. Paired with Brandie Burton, against Davies and Alison Nicholas, Mochrie yelled "Yes!" when Davies missed a short birdie putt and later refused to concede Davies a 12-inch putt on the 16th. When the Americans won 2 and 1, the bad manners became the story across the pond. "Dottie goes potty over mayhem in the mountains" cried a headline in The Observer.

Photo: David Cannon

JoAnne Carner's sequined cap drew much attention throughout the week, and now resides in her trophy case at Palm Beach National Golf Club, Lakeworth, Florida.

Photo: Stephen Munday

Laura Davies and Alison Nicholas defeated Betsy King (holding iron) and Donna Andrews 2 & 1 in opening day foursomes play.

Still smarting from the American's loss at Dalmahoy, Dottie (Pepper) Mochrie showed up with red hair and her "game face" at the Opening Ceremonies.

"THEY SAY BLONDES HAVE MORE FUN, BUT REDHEADS ARE MORE FIERY."

USA Captain JoAnne Carner, commenting on Dottie's red hair.

The Greenbrier Professional Emeritus Samuel Jackson Snead was on hand for the action during the entire week.

"I don't really care," said a defiant Mochrie. "I know what it takes for me to play well. I know I'm professional about it. I don't get in anybody's way. And I have to be happy with myself first and foremost."

The controversial match set the stage for the final day of 10 singles matches. The Europeans were still the looser squad, but the Americans showed in their team dinner on Saturday night that they were catching Carner's spirit. The usually shy Daniel made an emotional speech, and at the end drew roars when she pointed to her captain and declared, "And just remember, it isn't over till the fat lady holds the Cup."

Things began tentatively with King, who had short putting problems, beaten by Helen Alfredsson. But in the second match, Mochrie backed up her Tony Montana stance by making seven birdies in 13 holes to steamroll Catrin Nilsmark 6 and 5. "That's the best golf I've ever seen," Nilsmark told Mochrie, who finished the Cup 3-0. More importantly, the sequential posting of her rout on the scoreboards seemed to give courage to her teammates, who went on to win seven of the next eight matches, bringing the final score to 13-7.

With the Cup regained, Carner finally allowed herself to show the strain. "It was like I played every shot, I putted every putt, I hit every chip," she confessed. "I've got a headache, and I'm ready for a Stoli." Yeah, even Big Momma was nervous at The Greenbrier.

Members of the European Team sportingly wore American flags to the Closing Ceremonies.

Photo: David Cannon

"LAKE NONA WAS A LOW-KEY AFFAIR COMPARED TO THIS ONE.
I MEAN, THIS ONE HAS JUST BEEN ENORMOUS WITH HUGE GALLERIES,
LITERALLY HUNDREDS OF THE WORLD'S PRESS, AND TELEVISION ALL
ACROSS THE WORLD." European Captain Mickey Walker

1994 TEAMS

USA		EUROPE	
JoAnne Carner, Captain	Washington	Mickey Walker, Captain	England
Donna Andrews	Virginia	Helen Alfredsson	Sweden
Brandie Burton	California	Laura Davies	England
Beth Daniel	South Carolina	Lora Fairclough	England
Tammie Green	Ohio	Trish Johnson	England
Betsy King	Pennsylvania	Liselotte Neumann	Sweden
Meg Mallon	Massachusetts	Alison Nicholas	England
Dottie (Pepper) Mochrie	New York	Catrin Nilsmark	Sweden
Kelly Robbins	Michigan	Dale Reid	Scotland
Patty Sheehan	Vermont	Annika Sorenstam	Sweden
Sherri Steinhauer	Wisconsin	Pam Wright	Sweden

Photo: David Cannon

"JoAnne was an inspiration. We would sit around in team meetings and she would tell us war stories. She really fired us up."

Donna Andrews

Photo: David Cannon

1996

St. Pierre Hotel Golf & Country Club

Tales of Wales and a 10–2 Sunday romp

BY DAVID DAVIES

Photo: David Cannon

★ ★ ★

Sunday Sept. 22, 1996, St. Pierre Hotel Golf & Country Club, Chepstow, Wales: a date and place due to be inscribed in golf's history books. Europe, already the holders of the Ryder Cup, the Curtis Cup and the Walker Cup were about to win The Solheim Cup to create an altogether different Impregnable Quadrilateral, a quite glorious Grand Slam.

Never, in the history of competition between the United States and either, in the early days, Great Britain and Ireland, or latterly, Europe, had the latter team held all four of golf's great Cups. But on this salubrious September Sunday, that, it seemed, was about to change.

★ ★ ★

Galleries turned out early Sunday in anticipation of a European win, which was not to be.

"I'VE ALWAYS SAID WE'RE SLIGHT UNDERDOGS.
WE'RE PLAYING IN EUROPE." USA Captain Judy Rankin

Above right: Beth Daniel takes a fling with her PING as she accounted for $1^{1}/_{2}$ points in opening round play.

The European team had put in the hard yards in the four-ball and foursomes series and they had forged what is, in this match format, a priceless lead of 2 points with only the 12 singles to come.

Small though it may seem a margin of 9-7 is a lead any captain of any of those Cup teams would sell his or her soul for; a vital edge both actual and psychological as it means, in a 28 point match, that the leaders have to win only $5^{1}/_{2}$ of the 12 singles, the trailing team $7^{1}/_{2}$.

Furthermore, the Europeans, as a team, were quietly confident. Their supporters, nicknamed the Spontaneous Orpheus after the Welsh, and world-famous, Morriston Orpheus male voice choir just down the road, more vocally so.

All week a group, formed on an ad hoc basis, in the bleachers by the first tee, had been serenading the players as they arrived for their matches. Annika Sorenstam, or almost all the Swedes for that matter, was greeted with a rendition of the Abba song "Super Trooper," although, obviously, "What's it all about, Alfie?" was reserved for Helen Alfredsson.

Dale Reid was serenaded with "Flower of Scotland," and tugged in embarrassed fashion on her cigarette during it, and Marie Laure de Lorenzi had to endure a wordless, da da da da da da di di de dum version of her national anthem, "La Marseillaise." The Frenchwoman turned to the choir and pretended to conduct them and confessed afterwards that for a collection of "rosbifs"–the French slang word for Roast Beef and also for the British–the singing had not been too bad.

England's Laura Davies and Lisa Hackney scored a convincing 6 & 5 win over Beth Daniel and Val Skinner in Saturday's four-ball competition, helping Europe to a 9-7 lead at the end of the day.

"PROFESSIONAL GOLF IS ALL ABOUT SUNDAY AFTERNOON IN EVERY TOURNAMENT WE PLAY. THE SOLHEIM CUP AND RYDER CUP ARE NO DIFFERENT." Laura Davies

Annika Sorenstam seldom missed a fairway during the week, scoring the most points of any player. She was the only European to win a Sunday singles match.

The European captain, Mickey Walker, who had to wear an eye patch after an unfortunate brush with a wasp, was greeted on the tee with the theme music from the film "The Sting" and even the BBC reporter Maureen Madill, who had played Curtis Cup golf on this very course, was met with "When Irish Eyes are Smiling."

It was fun, it was properly managed in that it did not spill over into the players preparation to play and was entirely appropriate to the host country, Wales, often called the Land of Song.

There was optimism in the air, then, as far as Europe was concerned and it was time for the American captain, Judy Rankin, to summon the sinews of her team. Not that she needed any dramatic declarations, no readings from the Alamo, nothing of the fist-pumping, bulging-eyed variety of speech making in the team room.

She knew the calibre of her players, knew that each of them was, on her day, capable of beating anyone and perhaps most of all she knew how they felt at being 9-7 down. "We had expected the match to be close," she said later, "but we had not expected to be down going into the singles. That gave everyone a bit of a shock and everyone came out so determined."

There were, of course, a great many factors in favour of the visiting team. Week in, week out they played on by far the strongest tour in the world, they were accustomed to being in contention and therefore to playing their golf under pressure.

All 12 of the team were in the top 21 of the world rankings while the Europeans could only manage six at that level, with the remainder stretching from 22nd to 97th. It was one thing for Captain Walker to talk about her "great" European players, but in reality there was only Laura Davies, then number one in the world, Annika Sorenstam and, just possibly, Alison Nicholas, in that category.

The Welsh countryside provided a compelling panorama for a Saturday four-ball match.

Photo: Stephen Munday

Trish Johnson bombs a tee shot as she and Laura Davies scored a lopsided 6 & 5 win over Kelly Robbins and Pat Bradley.

USA supporters stood out in the predominantly European gallery.

"ALL THE MATCHES ARE IMPORTANT, BUT I THOUGHT BEATING LAURA WOULD GIVE THE OTHERS A BIT OF CONFIDENCE."

Michelle McGann

In contrast the visitors could call on any number of proven great players. Pat Bradley, Beth Daniel, Betsy King, Dottie Pepper, Meg Mallon - any side with those players as its spine would have backbone enough for any match. The Americans, then, knew they should win; it was just a matter of proving it.

When the singles order was announced there was, at least in the European quarter of the media center, the first hint of disquiet, a little unease. Laura Davies, who loves The Solheim Cup as no other golfing event, had been playing, in the words of Dottie Pepper, "like a runaway train."

It was an apt description of a player who likes nothing better than to race round the golf course, spending minimal time over her shots causing her opponents to become breathless not just at her ability but also in the simple act of keeping up.

In a singles order in a Cup match there is only one place for a Laura, and that is at the top. Let her lead by example, steaming ahead at the front and, in theory anyway, inspiring the lesser lights lower down the order. But Walker, for some reason that was never explained, decided to put Davies out at no. 3, so slowing down and generally inhibiting her most inspirational player.

Sorenstam was at no. 1 and in pure golf terms, inarguably so. But a Sorenstam victory - and she went on to beat Pat Bradley 2 & 1 - is a death by a thousand cuts in comparison to the sabre charge of a Davies. The Swede is a wonderful player but she cannot ignite a crowd like the Englishwoman can and all that came from ahead was the polite applause that she extracts from her galleries, as against the roars a charging Davies might have produced.

In fact, this was a Sunday when those joyful voices around the first tee were quickly stilled. It was a Sabbath more notable for its silence as the leader board showed the red numbers used for the American team becoming predominant. The crowds were not anti-USA, more depressed at the poor showing of a home team that had flattered, but only ultimately to deceive. It was not, in the end, even a contest.

Annika walked a lonely path at the top of the order and when she won, gave her team a 10-7 lead. No one knew it then, of course, but that was to be the last match that Europe won in the 1996 Solheim Cup. There were to be two halved matches later on but the rest of it was a picture perfect display from the American team of how to cope with the severest pressure.

The second European out was, rather surprisingly, Kathryn Marshall, and her match attracted practically no crowd at all. The Scot was actually unlucky in that she was one of only three players of the home team to be under par when her match ended but her opponent, Val Skinner, at 4-under, was 2-better - a fact that owed something to two outrageous bounces. Twice her shots headed straight at some of the lovely oaks, many of them over 100 years old, that line the St. Pierre fairways, and twice they hit the trees and bounced back into the fairway.

Photo: David Cannon

Their first victory on European soil was enjoyed by Captain Judy Rankin and her USA team.

USA's Meg Mallon posted a win and three halved matches at St. Pierre to go undefeated.

1996 St. Pierre Hotel Golf & Country Club   75

But you have to make the most of chances like that. Skinner did, and the remainder of the singles series was little more than a procession. Davies, as predicted, struggled with the pace of play and at one point, the 309 yards long par 4 8th, irritably smashed a huge drive within a few feet of the green while Marshall and Skinner were still on it.

It availed her nothing and Michelle McGann strolled, literally, to a 3 & 2 win. "I didn't want to be rushed," she said, "and I wasn't."

With the home team heroine safely despatched, the remaining matches were, to European eyes, embarrassing. Liselotte Neumann managed a half with Beth Daniel as did Nicholas with Kelly Robbins but for the remainder the leader boards were drowned in a red sea. In the singles America as a team were 13-under par; Europe were 20-over. The visitors had won by the crushing margin of 17-11.

History, it became apparent, was going to have to wait a while. All four cups on the eastern edge of the Atlantic was not for now. But perhaps there had been some hint of that on Sunday morning in St. Pierre's tiny, centuries old church at the back of the regular 18th green. Alison Nicholas, a committed Christian, read the early morning service lesson which came from 1 Corinthians 9, verses 24-25 and, in part, read: "Know ye not that they which run in a race run all, but one receiveth the prize."

"So run, that ye may obtain."

But races, of course, invariably go to the swift and on Sunday Sept. 22 the Americans were by far the fleetest of foot.

Val Skinner (2-2-0) and Jane Geddes (1-2-1) earned their spots on the USA Team at St. Pierre, the only Solheim Cup in which they would participate.

A braid and a bow added a colorful flair to Michelle McGann's hairdo during Friday's opening round play.

EUROPE		USA	
Mickey Walker, Captain	England	Judy Rankin, Captain	Texas
Helen Alfredsson	Sweden	Pat Bradley	Massachusetts
Laura Davies	England	Brandie Burton	California
Marie-Laure de Lorenzi	France	Beth Daniel	South Carolina
Lisa Hackney	England	Jane Geddes	New York
Trish Johnson	England	Rosie Jones	California
Kathryn Marshall	Scotland	Betsy King	Pennsylvania
Joanne Morley	England	Meg Mallon	Massachusetts
Liselotte Neumann	Sweden	Michelle McGann	Florida
Alison Nicholas	England	Dottie Pepper	New York
Catrin Nilsmark	Sweden	Kelly Robbins	Michigan
Dale Reid	Scotland	Patty Sheehan	Vermont
Annika Sorenstam	Sweden	Val Skinner	Montana

Photo: David Cannon

1996 St. Pierre Hotel Golf & Country Club　　77

The Ohio University marching band struts its stuff.

Photo: David Cannon

1998

Muirfield Village Golf Club

At the house that Jack built

BY LISA D. MICKEY

Photo: Tom Able Green

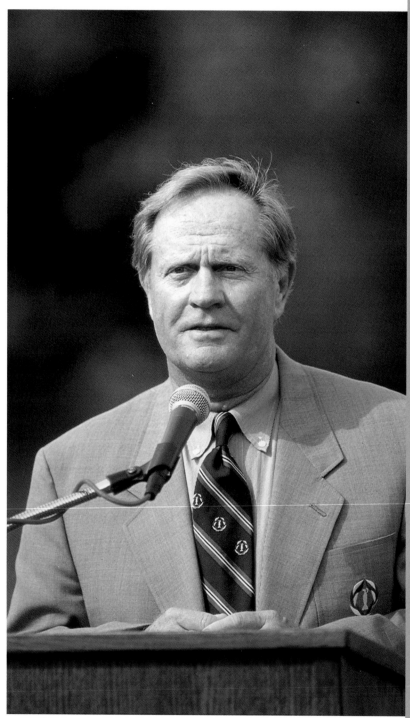

Jack Nicklaus

★ ★ ★

The time had come.

Time for the women's golf event with the most public pizzazz to grow up. Time for The Solheim Cup to register on the radar of every sports junkie's brain and every sentimental golf fan's heart. Time for The Solheim Cup to become recognized and accepted as more than a scaled-down, female version of the Ryder Cup.

And with a roster on each side loaded with star-quality talent from the United States and Europe, and packed with a more eclectic collection of personalities than a Juilliard drama class, galleries at The 1998 Solheim Cup walked into a golf event that bubbled over into something more akin to one of those Ohio Saturday-afternoon football frenzies.

This fifth staging of the biennial match-play clash between teams on either side of the Atlantic had already logged its time of growth and sometimes seemingly snail's-pace maturation. The Solheim Cup opened with no fanfare in 1990, and spent the next several years seeking the necessary footing to prove itself as something more than a marketing tool for a brilliant clubmaker - PING founder Karsten Solheim - and more than a warm-and-fuzzy engagement between two sides of women professionals still trying to earn respect in the niche world of tour golf and the painted corner of women's sports.

★ ★ ★

Attendance records for The Solheim Cup were set every day of the competition, as well as the Opening and Closing Ceremonies.

"THE FACT THAT JACK (NICKLAUS) INVITED US HERE IS HUGE FOR THE SOLHEIM CUP. NOT THAT IT NEEDED ANY MORE CREDIBILITY, BUT IT DID ADD CREDIBILITY, TOOK US TO ANOTHER LEVEL." Laura Davies

The brothers Solheim—Karsten Louis, John and Allan—catch
opening day action which saw the USA take a commanding
$5^1/_2$ to $2^1/_2$ lead.

By the time The Solheim Cup arrived at Muirfield
Village Golf Club in Dublin, Ohio – welcomed with
the blessings of no other than course designer Jack
Nicklaus himself – the stage had been set for something larger than this event had ever known. Every
player who set foot on Jack's turf felt the tingle of
expectancy the minute she walked to her first match
on the first tee. They felt it when the flags of participating nations clanked up their poles. And they felt it
when fans poured through the gates with the same
fervor and anticipation that came here for the 1987
Ryder Cup and the PGA Tour's annual Memorial
Tournament.

But this time, it wasn't the history of PGA players
before them that jangled the nerve endings of these
U.S. and European women players. Instead, it was
the belief that this storied venue would become the
new stage for the new age of all Solheim Cups to follow. If a world-class kickoff was what the fans came
to see, by golly, these two teams of 12 players would
deliver. And for those wondering if women could
play this course long associated with the best in
men's golf, that matter was settled by Sunday's
Closing Ceremonies.

"It was such a terrific venue with two great
teams, crowds of knowledgeable people and the vil-
las on site where players lived together for the
week," said Juli Inkster, playing in the second of her
five Cup appearances for the U.S. "It felt like The
Solheim Cup had arrived and I think the Europeans
felt it, too. The place gave me goose bumps. Just
walking to the first tee, with everybody lined up and
fans from both sides singing their songs, I was the
most nervous I'd ever been. I had cotton mouth. It
was just electric out there."

Judy Rankin could become the only undefeated, two-time champion captain in Solheim Cup history.

"THIS IS WHAT WE PLAY FOR. THIS IS FOR NO MONEY. THIS IS ALL FOR PRIDE."

Juli Inkster

European Captain Pia Nilsson takes the stage to introduce her team.

The day before the first matches, Inkster and her two daughters - Hayley, then 8, and Cori, then 4 - were picked by U.S. team Captain Judy Rankin to raise the American flag at Opening Ceremonies. Even Inkster, a perpetual jokester, got a lump in her throat when it came time to hoist Old Glory.

And then it was time for the teams to raise their clubs in three days of teeth-bared competition. That unbridled nationalism often morphed into comedic moments of combined frustration and venting by players from both sides. It no longer mattered that this same group of players largely saw each other week after week on the LPGA Tour. The Solheim Cup elicited emotions not normally found at regular tour events, prompting typically thick skins to develop acute sensitivity to everything from fist pumps to pumped fists into punching bags bearing targeted players' faces.

"It was all in good fun," said Laura Davies of the leak that a few members of the European team had taken pokes at a punching bag bearing the photo of Dottie Pepper.

"She's just a target in that setting," said U.S. team captain, Judy Rankin. "There was a lot of carping about Dottie. You can be more vocal in a team atmosphere and Dottie was vocal. That kind of intensity always helped her play better and it also helped her teammates."

When the 1998 Cup began, the Americans led the event's series with three Cup wins and one loss. When this Cup was complete, the U.S. had improved its record to 4-1 with a 16-12 three-day cumulative total. But it was not without a fight, especially by Pepper, who went undefeated in the event and unfazed by her opponents' sniping. Truth is, Pepper put on her game face driving to Muirfield and took it off only to laugh her way out of the gates.

Laura Davies posted a 3-1-1 record at Muirfield Village, the best among European players.

Photo: Rob Griffin

Photographers are guaranteed an exciting day when they follow Dottie
Pepper with a camera. She was top USA point-earner on a 4-0-0 record.

Photo: Rob Griffin

Juli Inkster holes Dottie Pepper's drive at #17 in their 3 & 1 win over Laura Davies and Trish Johnson.

Annika Sorenstam played in every match and posted a 3-2 record for the week.

"WE FOUGHT SO HARD, AND WE WANTED THE CUP SO BADLY."

Annika Sorenstam

The Europeans had their own stalwarts in a team nucleus built around Laura Davies, Alison Nicholas and Trish Johnson, alongside six Swedes - including then-rising star Annika Sorenstam and super-spirited Helen Alfredsson, who was the European equivalent of the Yanks' Pepper on the intensity chart. But there were times when the emotional pot boiled over.

When Pepper and Inkster faced Alfredsson and Marie-Laure de Lorenzi in the second day's foursomes, the Americans had a 50-foot putt, which they knocked to within $1^1/_2$ feet. Instead of telling the Americans to mark the ball before they played their chip to the green, the Europeans told the Yanks to pick up. When the Americans picked up their ball, the gallery erupted into what sounded like a touchdown in a packed stadium.

"They made a match-play mistake," said Inkster. "They should have made us mark it. I walked back to Dottie after that long putt, raised my hand and said to her, 'How about that?' And the crowd just went crazy."

The Euros chipped, missed and lost the match. And much was said about the fan response to Pepper and Inkster's greenside celebration.

Featuring a low center of gravity, Tammie Green played 6 months pregnant, the first such player to do so in The Solheim Cup.

Inkster got a second adrenaline rush later that afternoon when she teamed with Meg Mallon in their four-ball match against Liselotte Neumann and Charlotta Sorenstam. The Americans were 1-up when they arrived at the 17th green. In perhaps the event's most dramatic hole, four players gutted out a memorable sequence of events.

"Liselotte was in the bunker about 40 feet away and she hit one of the greatest bunker shots I've ever seen to six inches," said Rankin.

The gallery once again erupted and the Europeans looked to be in good position as the Americans hovered behind their 45-foot putt for birdie. Mallon advised Inkster to get the speed right.

"I let it go and I thought, 'This looks good. This looks good. THIS LOOKS GOOD!' And it went in," said Inkster, whose putt gave them a 2-up win. "That was a match-play bomb."

The week was full of moments punctuated by what sounded like bowl games scattered throughout Muirfield's 220 acres. There were on-course comic moments, such as when the U.S. team's Brandie Burton took a mighty swipe at one awkward sidehill shot and landed in a creek.

Laughter resounded through the trees as Burton's caddie dug her lost shoe out of the mud. Burton never complained about the injury that would later result in two ankle surgeries.

Former U.S. captain and LPGA Hall of Famer Kathy Whitworth walked in the gallery along the ropes beneath a giant American flag. Australian star Karrie Webb showed up to cheer for friends on the U.S. team. And Tammie Green, plodding along dutifully on the turf of her home state, became the first woman to win her Solheim Cup singles match while playing pregnant. Green beat Europe's Alison Nicholas 1 up.

A U.S. captain's pick, Sherri Steinhauer went on to validate Rankin's choice by winning her match 3 and 2 against Catriona Matthew to clinch the Americans' team title. With the Cup's win safely secured for the U.S., the final stage had been set for the moment that most defined the '98 Cup.

Walking down the 18th fairway in Sunday's final match with galleries stretched the length of the hole, Mallon conceded the last hole to wildcard Sophie Gustafson to halve the match. The gesture caught the rookie by surprise and drew long, appreciative applause by fans who understood.

"When Meg said, 'I'm giving you that putt,' I wasn't sure if she expected me to give her her putt," said Gustafson, looking back. "But I soon figured it out. It was a great gesture by Meg and people still remember it. What I remember most, though, wasn't so much about playing golf, but being a part of something that big."

And big, it was. The Solheim Cup had arrived and parity between the two sides was taking shape, setting the stage for future clashes. The groundwork was laid in 1998 for a world-class women's golf event over at Jack's place, and The Solheim Cup has never been the same since that September weekend in Ohio.

Photo: Rob Griffin

Meg Mallon

Photo: Rob Griffin

Sophie Gustafson

"BUT I SOON FIGURED IT OUT. IT WAS A GREAT GESTURE BY MEG AND PEOPLE STILL REMEMBER IT. WHAT I REMEMBER MOST, THOUGH, WASN'T SO MUCH ABOUT PLAYING GOLF, BUT BEING PART OF SOMETHING THAT BIG." Sophie Gustafson

USA supporters strike a Sunday silhouette at the conclusion of the match.

1998 TEAMS

USA	
Judy Rankin, Captain	Texas
Donna Andrews	Virginia
Brandie Burton	California
Tammie Green	Ohio
Pat Hurst	California
Juli Inkster	California
Chris Johnson	California
Rosie Jones	California
Betsy King	Pennsylvania
Meg Mallon	Massachusetts
Dottie Pepper	New York
Kelly Robbins	Michigan
Sherri Steinhauer	Wisconsin

EUROPE	
Pia Nilsson, Captain	Sweden
Helen Alfredsson	Sweden
Laura Davies	England
Marie-Laure de Lorenzi	France
Sophie Gustafson	Sweden
Lisa Hackney	England
Trish Johnson	England
Catriona Matthew	Scotland
Liselotte Neumann	Sweden
Alison Nicholas	England
Catrin Nilsmark	Sweden
Annika Sorenstam	Sweden
Charlotta Sorenstam	Sweden

Photo: David Cannon

"I ALWAYS WONDERED WHAT IT WOULD BE LIKE WALKING UP THE 18TH HOLE AND FEELING THE STADIUM EFFECT OF THIS GOLF COURSE." Tammie Green

Photo: Courtesy of Loch Lomond Golf Club

2000

Loch Lomond Golf Club

On the bonnie, boggy Scottish banks

BY DEREK LAWRENSON

Photo: Stuart Franklin

Former LPGA Commissioner Charles S. Mechem Jr. extends condolences to members of the Solheim family on the passing of PING Founder Karsten Solheim earlier in the year.

★ ★ ★

No one who was there will ever forget the stygian conditions in which the sixth Solheim Cup was played. There is a very good reason why Loch Lomond is referred to as the bonnie, bonnie banks but anyone turning up for the first time that week would have had great difficulty peering through the endless gloom to discover it.

For this Solheim Cup to be remembered for something other than the weather, therefore, required performances of remarkable skill, patience, and desire. To the surprise of many who had witnessed three comfortable victories in succession for the United States, it was the Europeans who were not found wanting when it came to these fundamental qualities.

By pulling off their astonishing against-all-odds success, the home side moved The Solheim Cup from the realms of a pleasurable occasion to a contest in all forms of the word. True, it was not their first victory, but it was the one that demonstrated that generations would not pass between each triumph. "The goal was to make The Solheim Cup a first-class event," said Annika Sorenstam, and how gloriously it was achieved. Henceforth, the match took on all the characteristics of big brother, the Ryder Cup, enveloping all who played and all who watched in its searing, captivating vice.

★ ★ ★

Laura Davies found the pot of gold at the end of the rainbow, playing on her 6th consecutive Solheim Cup team.

"I THINK WE'RE READY TO GO. THERE'S NOT A MEMBER OF OUR TEAM ON ANY GIVEN WEEK WHO COULD NOT WIN ANYWHERE IN THE WORLD." Laura Davies

The principals of Lyle Anderson Company, owners of Loch Lomond GC, join Solheim Cup players and captains on the steps of Rossdhu House. Left to right are Phil Schneider, Lyle and Missy Anderson, Sally and Rich Lehmann and Phil Edlund.

To the players, then, all the credit for producing such pivotal drama. Praise as well to the main characters in the sub-plot, the 60-strong greens staff, who must have spent many of the 72 hours during that long, long weekend wondering what on earth they had done for nature to be so cruel.

The cruel one in the build-up was the European Captain Dale Reid, or at least that was how she was painted by her critics. How on earth could the Scot leave out the golden girl from her homeland, Catriona Matthew? How could she go with Swedes like Helen Alfredsson, who had all the experience-but no form? "Just a hunch," explained Reid, and on hunches, of course, are some of the greatest captaincy decisions made.

Reid was not the only one who was vilified. Her entire team paled when held under the harsh light given out by their talented opponents. The press wanted to know: isn't it time the Europeans were augmented with the best of the Koreans, the Aussies, indeed anyone who would fight tooth and fingernail? Dottie Pepper, never at the back of the line when it comes to throwing fat on fire, was quoted as saying that the Europeans "would be packing groceries somewhere" if it was not for the LPGA Tour. The bookmakers in the UK agreed with the hostile press, making the visitors prohibitive favourites.

Lift, clean and place was the order of the week as Solheim Cuppers took measures to keep dry, especially France's Patricia Meunier-Lebouc.

*"I*T WAS RAINING AND WAS FOGGY, BUT FOR US IT WAS SUNSHINE THE WHOLE WEEK. IF YOU GET IN THE RIGHT MOOD IT'S FUNNY WHAT THAT CAN DO." Helen Alfredsson

Thanks to umbrellas, towels and an efficient caddy, Pat Hurst stayed dry enough to post a successful 2-1-1 record at Loch Lomond.

All this might have had an unsettling effect on some but it was like water off a rhino to the European talisman, Laura Davies. She gave a hint of the intensity in the home locker room when she said: "It's good to be told you're not good enough. It makes you bitter."

On the eve of the matches, Sorenstam - yes, shy, retiring Annika - stood up at the team meeting and told everyone it was ridiculous to be portrayed as inferior. "We have 100 tournament wins in this room," she said. "We have enough career prize money to buy half this island."

Jack Nicklaus' sixth Masters victory in 1986 might be the most notable instance of when a player used criticism as an unsparing, motivating force - the Golden Bear stuck an article claiming he was washed up on his refrigerator door at the start of the week - but this ran it close.

And so Reid knew exactly who she wanted standing on the first tee in the first match. She knew who would turn her face against the press, the Americans and the elements, who would get the crowd wrapped up from the opening drive and act like an impenetrable barrier between her team and their opponents.

Good old Laura, paired with long-time buddy Alison Nicholas, and Davies was happiness itself when she realized the opposition would be provided by Pepper, and her playing partner, Juli Inkster.

Umbrellas became a 15th weapon in everyone's golf bag throughout the week as Carin Koch will attest.

Husband Fredrik and daughter Tuva share in the joy of Catrin Nilsmark's undefeated (3-0-0) play at Loch Lomond.

Dottie Pepper and Juli Inkster lost their opening foursomes match but would bounce back with singles victories on Sunday.

"THIS IS THE BEST AGAINST THE BEST."

Captain Pat Bradley on opening day's first match: Davies/Nicholas vs. Pepper/Inkster

It is interesting to look back on that opening foursomes series from a distance, to see the way each match was closer in turn but each ended in victory for the home side. Here was a prime example of the importance of momentum. Davies and Nicholas got ahead early - they were three up after four - as did Trish Johnson and Sophie Gustafson in the second game. Those who came behind looked at leader-boards and all they saw was blue.

Imagine how much easier it must have been for the all-Swede pairing of Catrin Nilsmark and Carin Koch, coming down the stretch all square in their own match but possessing the psychological comfort of knowing that two points were already in the bag. And how much easier again for the all-blond-haired-blue-eyed pairing of Sorenstam and Janice Moodie, when two points had become three.

When these two wrapped up victory on the home hole against Meg Mallon and Beth Daniel, it was the first time in Solheim Cup history that a series had ended in a whitewash for either side. The fact it was the Europeans who were doing the whitewashing made it all the more astonishing, of course, but the urge the home players must have felt to hose their critics was tempered by the knowledge that the finishing line was still a league in the distance.

Johnson warned that the Americans "would be out for blood this afternoon," and so they were, quickly claiming the prized scalp of Davies and Nicholas, who were emotionally spent. The Americans had two and a half points out of three by the time Mallon and Daniel came down the last against Moodie and Sorenstam for the second time that day.

Janice Moodie and Annika Sorenstam celebrate winning Friday's fourth European point in 1-up win over Meg Mallon and Beth Daniel.

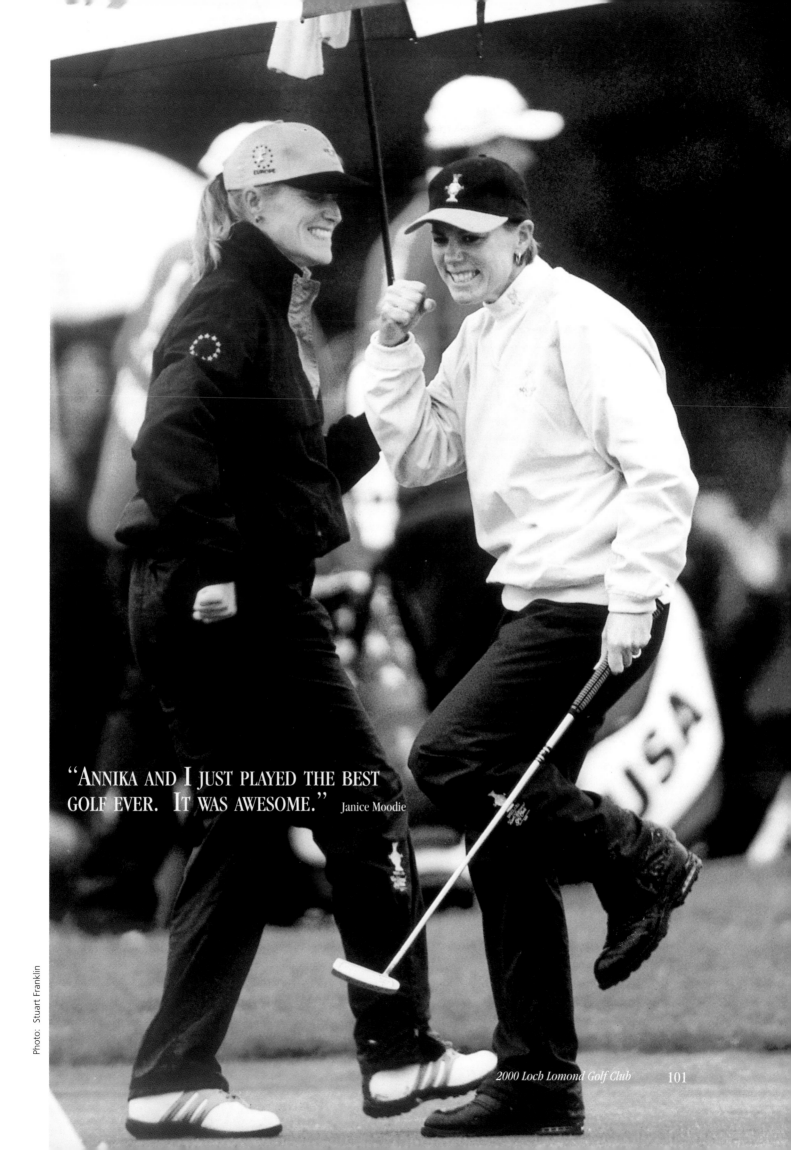

"ANNIKA AND I JUST PLAYED THE BEST GOLF EVER. IT WAS AWESOME." Janice Moodie

2000 Loch Lomond Golf Club 101

Now the psychological positions were totally reversed for the latter pair. The home side desperately needed a halve at the absolute worst if the morning's gains were not to be all but wiped out. Both teams hit fine drives but it was Mallon who faltered, the Americans who bogeyed the hole, and an important point had been claimed.

The Saturday of Solheim Cup week was one of those doleful days when you peek out the window at first light and know the rain is going to be unremitting. Five hundred miles to the south, the semi-finals of the men's World Matchplay Championship at Wentworth never got to the first tee.

At Loch Lomond, it was remarkable that two matches were played to a conclusion, and it was the home side who clutched both points. Four matches were suspended until the following morning, with Europe down in only one.

Clearly, the Americans would need the day of their lives to rescue this one.

What happened next might have totally overshadowed a lesser Solheim Cup than this one. Emerging into the murk the next morning came the warrior Sorenstam, playing a chip to perfection to rescue a losing situation against Kelly Robbins and Pat Hurst at the 13th.

But hold on a minute. Had Sorenstam not played out of turn, the Americans suddenly wanted to know. The referee was called and agreed that she had. What now? Given the dramatic nature of the shot, it would clearly take some chutzpah to ask her to play it again, even if it was fully within the rules. The Americans decided to leave that decision to their Captain Pat Bradley, who did just that.

Sorenstam would say later that she replayed it through the misty veil of her tears, and for weeks afterwards people would rage that Bradley had totally contravened the spirit of the game.

The Americans went on to win that hole, the match, and it was no consolation to Sorenstam that it was the only full point they claimed in the four-balls series. She played out the rest of The Solheim Cup with an empty heart.

Her teammates would rekindle her spirit by the close but not after a heart-stopping singles series. How could Europe lose a 9.5-4.5 lead? They almost did.

Captain Pat Bradley asks Annika Sorenstam to replay a holed chip shot, after the Swede had played out of turn.

Sweden's Sophie Gustafson had her "game face" on, an indicator that she was determined to win at Loch Lomond.

Photo: David Cannon

"WE WENT OUT AND PLAYED OUR HEARTS OUT," SAID MALLON. "WE ALMOST TOOK THIS THING, WHICH WOULD HAVE BEEN UNBELIEVABLE." Meg Mallon

So credit the Americans for making it so dramatic, for showing just why singles is their strongest suit. Here the momentum was all theirs.

Inkster wiped the floor with the sad Sorenstam. Brandie Burton demolished Sophie Gustafson. Pepper added a point and then so did Robbins. Suddenly the four points out of 12 that Europe needed from the singles looked a tall order indeed. At one point, there was so much red, white and blue on the leaderboard, that the teams were tied at 11.5 points each, with three matches still to emerge from the gloom.

It was Koch and Nilsmark, within seconds of each other, who turned the match back Europe's way. It was one of those occasions when you needed a split-screen. On the 18th green Nilsmark surveyed a birdie putt against Rosie Jones, while on the 17th, Koch was looking at a birdie putt to beat Michele Redman.

Within seconds of each other, the two Swedes accomplished their mission. Nilsmark rolled her putt up stone dead to force Jones to concede, just as Koch bolted hers into the hole. You had to feel for the Americans. "We went out and played our hearts out," said Mallon. "We almost took this thing, which would have been unbelievable."

So it would, but it was European smiles that beamed from the gloaming, a team that defied everyone and everything. Now the gloating could begin. "Do we still need all those international players?" Davies taunted the media. Talk about redemption day.

Carin Koch and Catrin Nilsmark won their Friday foursomes match, helping Europe to an unprecedented 4-0 sweep.

Photo: David Cannon

"I HAD A REALLY GOOD FEELING ALL DAY, AND IT WAS EXACTLY THE SAME FEELING I HAD IN DALMAHOY." Catrin Nilsmark

EUROPE		USA	
Dale Reid, Captain.	Scotland	Pat Bradley, Captain	Massachusetts
Pam Wright, Vice Captain	Scotland	Debbie Massey, Vice Captain	Michigan
Helen Alfredsson	Sweden	Brandie Burton	California
Raquel Carriedo	Spain	Beth Daniel	South Carolina
Laura Davies	England	Pat Hurst	California
Sophie Gustafson	Sweden	Juli Inkster	California
Trish Johnson	England	Becky Iverson	Michigan
Carin Koch	Sweden	Rosie Jones	California
Patricia Meunier-Lebouc	France	Meg Mallon	Massachusetts
Janice Moodie	Scotland	Dottie Pepper	New York
Liselotte Neumann	Sweden	Michele Redman	Ohio
Alison Nicholas	England	Kelly Robbins	Michigan
Catrin Nilsmark	Sweden	Nancy Scranton	Illinois
Annika Sorenstam	Sweden	Sherri Steinhauer	Wisconsin

Photo: Stuart Franklin

The Europeans celebrated late into the evening their second victory on Scottish soil.

"I'M SO PROUD OF MY PLAYERS. I COULDN'T BE HAPPIER. IT WAS A TOUGH FINAL DAY."

European Captain Dale Reid

Karsten Solheim

The man who made putters PINNNNG

BY JAMES ACHENBACH

Photo: Pete Samuels

I wish I had known Karsten Solheim in Redwood City, Calif., in the late 1950's, when PING became a reality, when all those scholarly, creative, fanciful ideas in his mind came leaping out in the form of a putter that would revolutionize golf.

I am captivated by the thought that each one of those early putters, assembled in his garage, literally had Karsten's fingerprints all over it.

What I would give to be transported back to that time. Karsten, who first played golf at 42 and was almost 50 when he manufactured the Redwood City putters, was about to emerge as an authentic golf genius.

Although Karsten was a late bloomer in golf, he would become recognized as the most influential golf club designer of the 20th century.

He had science on his side. His experience as an engineer with Ryan Aeronautical, Convair and General Electric didn't hurt. As a scientist, he was convinced that a heel-toe balanced putter would offer improved performance.

He was, of course, correct.

Despite his scientific background, his natural curiosity may have been his biggest asset. He wanted to know how things worked. He was always tinkering. He was constantly drawing up new concepts, such as the cabinet and rabbit ears antenna that clamped onto GE's first portable television.

PING will always be special in the sense that, as a company, it is a mirror reflection of Karsten and the intellect and principles that marked his life. He was a good man, and he was a generous man.

I miss him, even as I remind myself that his legacy is all around us. From Redwood City to Scottsdale, Ariz., to Phoenix, he blazed a trail that attracted a legion of friends, fans, followers, copycats and knockoff artists.

If the truth be told, not only is the PING EYE2 the biggest selling iron of all-time, but it also is the most copied iron in history. If imitation is a tribute, the PING Anser putter must be blushing after inspiring more look alikes than any putter ever made.

I was lucky in that eventually I did get to know Karsten, although he had already become famous and his clubs had become legendary.

I remember vividly the day I was sitting in Karsten's office, drinking tea with Karsten and his charming wife, Louise, when he suddenly jumped up, waved his arms in the air like some kind of magician, and walked directly toward his personal closet.

I knew this closet was full of experimental and prototype clubs that had never been produced, or had been bumped out of the PING lineup by another design, or had been declared nonconforming by the U.S. Golf Association.

Karsten and Sam Snead share a few laughs during Solheim Cup week at The Greenbrier.

Karsten set a new standard for wrangling with the USGA, although he always believed in the equitable creation and application of golf rules. He didn't argue, for example, when the USGA ruled against his bent shaft. Angled near the bottom of the grip, the shaft produced dramatic results when tested.

However, Karsten decided to take on both the USGA and PGA Tour over his shaping of so-called square grooves, or box grooves. He felt a ruling against his grooves was arbitrary and unfair, and he fought to prove it.

The USGA quickly settled with Karsten, avoiding a prolonged lawsuit, and the PGA Tour lawsuit ultimately resulted in a confidential settlement with Karsten. The results were hardly secret, as it became transparently clear that Karsten's argument had been acknowledged by the Tour.

Although box grooves are still with us today, they no longer are constructed in the shape that Karsten initiated. He agreed to this change after winning his showdown with the two organizations.

I reminisce about all this because the episode showed how dedicated and determined he could be. Karsten immersed himself in each and every project at PING.

As he opened his closet for me, I felt honored. More than 30 years of golf history lay in front of me. These clubs, too, had Karsten's fingerprints all over them.

He used his heel-toe concept in irons and eventually in woods. Almost single-handedly he brought high moment of inertia (resistance to twisting during the swing) to golf clubs. Before anyone else was doing it on a mass scale, he offered exotic grinds and bounces on PING wedges. More than anyone in the history of the game, he attempted to make putter heads and iron heads of different metals. When he needed a reliable golf-ball-hitting robot, he built his own, the PING man.

He could visualize, conceptualize, concoct and create. In other words, he could dream it and he could fabricate it. He could see it in his mind and he could manufacture it.

And he did all this with grace, dignity, pride and few words. He never led his own parade or blew his own horn. Heck he didn't even know what the horn looked like. All his life, he was humble and polite and sensitive.

Once again, I miss his demeanor. I miss his civility.

When I think of The Solheim Cup, I think of all these memories. Sometimes the greatest treasures live in our minds, to be rekindled and relived as often as we like.

If Ben Hogan had "the secret," Karsten had "the Anser," which really was simple enough: Be smart, be strong, be kind, be good.

He was.

Karsten met President Bill Clinton during USA Solheim Cup team visit to the White House following victory at The Greenbrier.

Photo: David Cannon

2002

Interlachen Country Club

Patty Berg, Bobby Jones and USA all the way

BY JOHN GARRITY

Photo: David Cannon

Photo: Rick Sharp

* * *

Odd, what you remember. I clearly recall a subdued Beth Daniel and Wendy Ward standing on a mound behind the eighteenth green at Interlachen Country Club after their Friday foursomes victory - the only U.S. victory of the morning. Daniel, an LPGA Hall of Famer, was trying to put some positive spin on the U.S. team's 1-3 start. "The first two days are basically exhibition golf," she said. "Whoever wins the singles usually wins The Solheim Cup."

She was right, of course. Almost half the points at a Solheim Cup are contested on Day Three, giving the 12 singles matches decisive weight. Interlachen would be no different. The U.S. team, trailing 9-7 after two days of foursome and four-ball play, would battle back in the Sunday singles to regain the Cup by a score of 15 $\frac{1}{2}$ to 12 $\frac{1}{2}$. "Singularly Superb!" crowed the headline in one golf weekly. "Sunday School!" echoed another.

Forgive me, but that's not how I remember the 2002 Solheim Cup. My version stars Laura Davies, the boisterous Englishwoman with the rugger's legs and publican's humor. It's Friday afternoon, and the clouds that have covered Minnesota all morning are giving way to sunshine. I'm following the first of the afternoon four-ball matches, which has Davies and the Spanish minx, Paula Marti, taking on Rosie Jones and Cristie Kerr. The Europeans are 4-down at the turn.

* * *

Laura Diaz was one of three USA players to register 3 points for her team.

"WHEN I WENT OUT FOR OUR FIRST MATCH FRIDAY WITH JULI, I DIDN'T KNOW IF THE RELATIONSHIP BETWEEN THE TWO TEAMS WOULD BE FRIENDLY OR CUTTHROAT. JULI SHOWED ME THAT IT'S VERY FRIENDLY." Laura Diaz

NBC-TV's David Bloom emceed Opening Ceremonies but lost his life in the war in Iraq seven months later.

Here's what I remember. Davies is in the right rough on the par-5 tenth hole, 270 yards from the flagstick. The situation is desperate, so she pulls the driver from her bag. I roll my eyes and shake my head, and I can only imagine what the TV analysts are saying. ("This ball could end up on Hubert Humphrey's headstone.") Anyway, Laura digs her spikes into the long grass, takes a huge swing with the driver, and blasts a screamer that bounces at the front of the green, scoots up the putting surface, races past the hole, and finally settles in the back fringe. The spectators give this shot about half its due - a smattering of yelps and whistles - but a few minutes later they produce a full-throated cheer when Davies rolls her putt into the hole for an eagle.

I remember that.

The picture gets a little hazy now, but I know from newspaper accounts that Davies birdied the par-5 thirteenth, reducing the Americans' lead to 2-up. The match is dormie on the seventeenth hole. Then, I remember, Davies sinks a 40-foot birdie putt to extend the match. Even the mosquitoes applaud.

Highlighting the Opening Ceremonies was a proud salute by the United States' premier bomber, the B-2 Spirit. It was the first fly-over by the plane at a golf tournament.

"IT'S STRESSFUL ENOUGH TRYING TO GET OUR TEAM RIGHT, WITHOUT TRYING TO GUESS WHAT PATTY'S GOING TO DO."

European Captain Dale Reid

Captains Dale Reid and Patty Sheehan wouldn't share their opening foursomes lineups until the appointed time.

So now we're on the tee of the eighteenth hole, a par 5 with a lake guarding the green. It's an historic hole. It's where in 1930 Bobby Jones hit his famous "lily pad shot," skipping his ball across the water on the way to victory in the U.S. Open, the third stage of his Grand Slam. Davies loves the eighteenth at Interlachen. "This is the ultimate set-up for me on a golf hole," she had said after pounding a huge drive to the edge of the water during her Friday morning foursomes victory (with Marti) over Juli Inkster and Laura Diaz. "If I were to design 18 holes just for me, this would be my finishing hole."

Or maybe just her ruin. Because this time a pumped-up Davies takes an aggressive line over the trees, wallops the ball high and long, and strides down the fairway as if she were Montgomery having just trounced Rommell ... only to discover that her ball has traveled 295 yards, bounced through the fairway, and gone into the drink.

I so remember her look of dismay.

Another thing I remember from Interlachen (I'll get back to loony Laura in a minute) is the wonderful fuss over remarks made a couple of weeks before by Europe's assistant captain, Catrin Nilsmark. Analyzing the U.S. team on a Swedish website, the stylish Nilsmark had called Kerr "a little brat," dismissed Ward as "too nice for match play," and said that Michele Redman had "absolutely no talent." (And those, she almost added, were their good points.) What the Europeans thought of their own team was less certain, but their captain, Dale Reid, produced the quote of the week when she explained why she couldn't pair Marti with her Spanish compatriot and fellow Solheim rookie, Raquel Carriedo. "They both speak Spanish," Reid said. "Just not to each other."

Laura Davies earned two points for the European Team, becoming the all-time leading point earner (16) in Solheim Cup competition, but didn't leave for home with the Cup.

Photo: David Cannon

"I CAN'T COMPLAIN ABOUT ANYTHING. I WAS THE FIRST TO HIT A SHOT IN THE 2002 SOLHEIM CUP AND I WAS A BIT NERVOUS. BUT AFTER THE FIRST HOLE, I WAS READY." Paula Marti

Photo: David Cannon

Wherever European fans gathered to cheer the action, Sweden's Helen Alfredsson could usually be found in the forefront.

"THE SOLHEIM CUP IS ONE OF THE MOST EXCITING THINGS I HAVE EVER DONE IN MY LIFE." *Carin Koch*

Photo: David Cannon

A hot putter permitted Sweden's Carin Koch to continue her unbeaten streak in Solheim Cup play at Interlachen CC, scoring 4.5 points.

I remember Sweden's pigtailed Carin Koch making putts from every point of the compass to lead both sides with $4\frac{1}{2}$ points. I remember Annika Sorenstam showing up on the first tee on an admittedly chilly Sunday morning in long pants, long sleeves, quilted vest, knit cap (pulled over the ears) and sunglasses, as if she were headed for the slopes at Vail. I remember U.S. captain Patty Sheehan praising the play of Laura Diaz, Kelli Kuehne, Emilee Klein, Kerr and Ward ("I've got some studmuffin pit-bull rookies out there"), and I remember her calling 42-year-old tour veteran Jones "my little rosebud." I even remember the turning point – the Sunday singles match between the great Sorenstam and Wendy "Too Nice" Ward, which ended with the disregarded former Curtis Cupper extracting a crucial half-point for the home team.

So why does my brain short out and scroll straight to Laura Davies and that Friday four-ball match? Wasn't it, as Daniel said, "exhibition golf?"

Left: Spain's Paula Marti opened with a foursomes win alongside Laura Davies but was not heard from again in the match.

Sure it was. But what an exhibition.

Davies, after a minute or so of pacing, clucking and tut-tutting over her bad fortune, drops a new ball in the fairway behind the water hazard. Lying two, she has 227 yards over water to the flag, and she has to get it close because Rosie Jones, playing the hole conventionally, is going to stick her third shot, with a wedge, five feet from the hole. (Marti and Kerr are spectators at this point, although they may remember it differently.) Davies pulls a long iron and stares across the water at the distant flag. She addresses the ball with a couple of aggressive waggles. She swings. And with all due respect to Bobby Jones, Laura doesn't need any water lilies to save her shot. Her ball clears the lake with room to spare and rolls to the back of the green, only fifteen feet from the hole.

I'm watching this, and I'm beginning to understand why Queen Elizabeth II named Davies a Commander of the Order of the British Empire. I'm also thinking that Laura Davies and match play are made for each other. She hits more truly awful shots in a week than most pros hit in a year, but she is blessed with power and guts and she loves the heroic carry, the go-for-broke flight of a ball over fen, bog or rooftop. "I am really happy to play with a legend like Laura," Marti would tell reporters at Interlachen. "She really helped me control the pressure out there."

Photo: David Cannon

Norway's Suzann Pettersen ponders a putt as she and Helen Alfredsson beat Kelly Robbins and Pat Hurst 4 & 2 in opening foursomes play.

Photo: David Cannon

Dottie Pepper qualified for the USA team but was unable to play because of injury.

Left: Wendy Ward took Annika Sorenstam to the 18th hole to gain a halve in their match.

Rosie Jones birdied the 18th to notch a 1 up win in afternoon four-balls with Christie Kerr over the Davies-Marti tandem.

Photo: David Cannon

"WE PRETTY MUCH SKIPPED UP THE FAIRWAY. I FELT MY JOB WAS DONE, AND WHEN I SAW MY TEAMMATES ON THE GREEN, IT WAS JUST A REALLY BIG RELIEF AND REAL PLEASURE." Rosie Jones

Anyway, Davies walks onto the eighteenth green to an ovation from the mostly-American gallery. She will later comment on the good sportsmanship of the crowd. "They're great," she'll say, "they're good natured. I've had so many Americans wish me luck, and it's genuine." At the moment, though, Davies is hoping to pound a stake into their collective heart. She has five paces of smooth green grass between her ball and the hole, and if she makes the birdie putt Rosie Jones will have to sink her five-footer to preserve a 1-up victory for the U.S.

Davies makes the putt.

There you have it, the 2002 Solheim Cup. Davies would leave Interlachen with a then-record 16 points in seven Solheim Cups - a nice stat to put on the mantle alongside her fifty or so international trophies. Asked on Saturday if it was her best Cup performance ever, she would say, "No question."

I remember that.

And I'll never forget the real ending of that Friday four-ball match. Little Rosie Jones - that "Rosebud" character - stepped up and holed her own birdie putt to halve the hole, frustrating Davies and saving the point for the Americans. "The look on Rosie's face when she needed to dig down deep and come up with something special," Kerr said afterwards, "I have never seen that in a regular tournament. It was truly special." An exuberant Captain Sheehan said, "That was one of the most awesome matches I have ever seen."

In the end, of course, the 2002 Solheim Cup was what Beth Daniel had predicted it would be – a singles shootout. The U.S. team prevailed on Sunday, 8 $\frac{1}{2}$ to 3 $\frac{1}{2}$, which was more than enough to deny the Europeans their first victory on American soil. "It was a funny week," Reid said. "There were so many ups and downs. I've never known a Solheim where fortunes turned around so much."

Solheim Cup rookie Cristie Kerr partnered Rosie Jones in her second match and the look on Rosie's face was "something special" that she had never witnessed in a regular tournament.

Photo: David Cannon

Honorary Interlachen CC member and LPGA Founder Patty Berg was the honorary chairperson for the 2002 event.

Photo: David Cannon

Too pooped to play, Laura Davies tired after 5 matches.   Photo: David Cannon

To be honest, I don't remember Reid saying that. But it was in the newspapers the next morning when the players and captains were catching their flights to Orlando, London, Phoenix, Madrid, San Francisco and Stockholm. What I do remember is the Sunday photograph of a dejected Davies sprawled on the ground at Interlachen, her chin supported on the heels of her hands. "A dejected Laura Davies," read the caption in one magazine, "termed the result 'miserable.'"

I would have chosen a different word: Unforgettable.

"THE AMERICANS ARE GREAT SUNDAY PLAYERS. WHILE THERE'S ALL THAT RED (ON THE SCOREBOARD), ALL YOU'RE REALLY TRYING TO DO IS WIN YOUR MATCH, BUT YOU CAN'T HELP JUST SEEING RED, RED, RED ALL THE WAY." Laura Davies

2002 TEAMS

USA		EUROPE	
Patty Sheehan, Captain	Vermont	Dale Reid, Captain	Scotland
Jane Geddes, Vice Captain	New York	Pam Wright, Vice Captain	Scotland
Beth Daniel	South Carolina	Helen Alfredsson	Sweden
Laura Diaz	New York	Raquel Carriedo	Spain
Pat Hurst	California	Laura Davies	England
Juli Inkster	California	Sophie Gustafson	Sweden
Rosie Jones	California	Maria Hjorth	Sweden
Cristie Kerr	Florida	Karine Icher	France
Emilee Klein	California	Carin Koch	Sweden
Kelli Kuehne	Texas	Paula Marti	Spain
Meg Mallon	Massachusetts	Mhairi McKay	Scotland
Michele Redman	Ohio	Suzann Pettersen	Norway
Kelly Robbins	Michigan	Annika Sorenstam	Sweden
Wendy Ward	Texas	Iben Tinning	Denmark

Members of the media swamp the victorious USA team.

Photo: David Cannon

Developed by Swedish entrepreneur Gösta Carlsson, Barsebäck G&CC provided a unique
combination of beautiful pine-lined fairways and links land.

Photo: Bergslagenbild AB

2003

Barsebäck Golf & Country Club

Sweden serves up tragedy & triumph

BY CARL MAGNUS HELLSTEN

Photo: David Cannon

Anna Lindh

9/11. September 11, 2003. Exactly two years after the terrorist attacks in New York and Washington D.C.,the Swedish minister of foreign affairs, Anna Lindh, dies at a hospital in Stockholm, the Capitol of Sweden. One day earlier Mrs. Lindh, without a bodyguard, was shopping at an exclusive downtown mall when she was attacked by a young man who stabbed her several times. She was so badly injured that the doctors could not save her life.

The tragedy that shocked Sweden took place less than 48 hours before The Solheim Cup opening ceremony at Barsebäck Golf & Country Club on the Swedish southwest coast.

Just hours after the Prime Minister Goran Persson, during a touching press conference, announced the death of Anna Lindh, the Swedish Captain of the European Solheim Cup team, Catrin Nilsmark, held a press conference at Barsebäck G&CC where she identified the players who will participate in the foursome matches on Friday morning.

Catrin Nilsmark explains why her fellow Swedes, the world's number one woman golfer Annika Sorenstam and Carin Koch won't play together and why she pairs Sorenstam together with the Norwegian talent Suzann Pettersen and Koch with England's giant Laura Davies. After the roster is released one reporter asks Catrin Nilsmark how she feels about the murder of Anna Lindh.

"I didn't know her in person but I'm a mother myself and to realize that two young sons have lost their mother is... devastating."

Says Catrin, wiping the tears from her cheek before she adds: "It has been a terrible day."

Several games in the Swedish Major soccer league are postponed out of respect for the minister's family, but what about The Solheim Cup? Could the event, which was supposed to be the perfect golf party with 100,000 spectators, really take place in a shocked nation?

After a meeting with the Solheim family, the President of the Swedish Golf Federation, Christer Orning, announces that The Solheim Cup will be played as planned.

John A. Solheim, Chairman and CEO of PING, explains why: "My mother Louise, myself and the rest of the Solheim family would like to express our deepest condolences, but we feel that playing The Solheim Cup is the best way to honour the murdered minister of foreign affairs Anna Lindh."

And thank God for that. The Solheim Cup 2003 became the golf tournament of the millennium for Sweden and this was a breathtaking week that we will never forget.

★ ★ ★

Drama unfolded daily at Barsebäck's signature 17th.

"THE CROWDS WERE SPECTACULAR AND I AM SO PROUD FOR BEING A SWEDE TO SEE SO MANY SWEDES OUT THERE." Annika Sorenstam

Above right: An awe inspiring salute by
Swedish Air Force "Team 60."

For weeks the Swedish press had followed the
European Solheim Cup Captain Catrin Nilsmark and
her state of health. Less than one week before the first
matches at Barsebäck, Catrin Nilsmark's husband had
to call 911 for an ambulance to take Mrs. Nilsmark to
the emergency room with severe back pain.

Will a hospitalized Nilsmark with a slipped disk
be able to lead the European team?

"Yes," says Catrin.

"Yes," says the Ladies European Tour
representatives.

The news in the world of golf was more about the
Captain's well-being rather than if the players were in
good shape and if the Captain had made the right
moves.

How energetic was Annika Sorenstam after
achieving her Grand Slam-career? Was it a good thing
to come to The Solheim Cup straight from a scuba-
diving vacation in Key Largo?

Did the Captain use her five wild cards correctly?
Shouldn't the Swedish major winner, Helen
Alfredsson, get one card for all that she has done for
Swedish and international golf?

Is it appropriate that a pregnant player (four
months) such as Patricia Meunier-Lebouc participate
in The Solheim Cup? Catrin Nilsmark thought so, and
the Captain was impressed by the French star's victory
in the major Kraft Nabisco Championship and the top-
10-finish at the Weetabix Women's British Open. Was
it right to hand out the last wild card to Janice
Moodie instead of Becky Morgan who had performed
quite well on the LPGA Tour?

Photo: David Cannon

"IT'S JUST THAT THESE THREE DAYS THEY
PLAYED BETTER. IF WE PLAYED NEXT WEEK
AND PLAYED FOR THREE DAYS, WE'D
PROBABLY WIN." Juli Inkster

A lot of experts in the media proved skeptical to the captain's picks but Catrin Nilsmark's roster was praised by the opponents.

Says the American "super-mom" Juli Inkster: "This European team is one of the best that I have ever played against. Catrin Nilsmark has done a great job as a captain. No doubt about that."

The American squad and several of the European players arrive at the local airport aboard a chartered plane from Oklahoma and the Williams Championship in Tulsa. It's a pretty long flight over the Atlantic Ocean but the European Captain Catrin Nilsmark probably had the toughest trip to Barsebäck. Because of the slipped disk, Catrin Nilsmark could not sit down on an airplane and take the one-hour flight from Stockholm to the southwest part of Sweden. Instead she lays in the trunk of the families' old Chevrolet Caprice Classic during the six-hour drive across the country. At last the injured captain arrives at Barsebäck where she jumps around on her crutches.

"Everywhere you go, always take the weather with you"... seems to be the melody for the European Captain. At Dalmahoy 1992 and at Loch Lomond 2000 the weather was really poor, with strong winds and heavy rain. Those are the only times that Europe has won The Solheim Cup.

Photo: Warren Little

She had all the bases covered for a European victory!

Photo: Scott Halleran

Photo: David Cannon

Swedish galleries totaled 100,000 for the week.

So now, Catrin Nilsmark wants to take the weather from Dalmahoy and Loch Lomond with her to Barsebäck.

Maybe the morning fog this Friday is a good sign for Europe. Half an hour after the first tee off (Laura Davies/Carin Koch v. Beth Daniel/Kelly Robbins) the fog is too thick and the play is temporarily put on hold.

The conditions turn from mostly overcast and hazy to a beautiful day that makes you feel that summer is on its way back even though fall is just around the corner. The interruption delays the schedule and when the night comes the scoreboard shows "Europe $4\frac{1}{2}$ and USA $3\frac{1}{2}$."

> "IT WAS DEFINITELY WORTH THE WAIT. JUST TO BE LUCKY ENOUGH TO BE IN THE MATCH THAT WON IT WAS AMAZING."
>
> Catriona Matthew

It's late Saturday. There is only one match that still hasn't finished. The four foursome matches before lunch gave Europe a 3-1 advantage but in the three four-ball matches in the afternoon the US fought back and won two of them. The last match is now on the 17th green and Annika Sorenstam has to make a 22-foot putt to halve the hole, and she does. Sorenstam and her partner Suzann Pettersen are now all square, with the Americans Laura Diaz and Kelly Robbins heading for the 18th tee.

The Barsebäck course concludes with a tough and decisive par 4 (393 yards) - a strong dogleg right which demands a long and precise drive. The closer you dare to hit your shot along the trees on the right side of the dogleg corner, the easier your approach shot will be. It's a great chance for a birdie and many matches could be decided here.

Errant drives contributed to several USA losses.

EUROPE	
Catrin Nilsmark, Captain	Sweden
Alison Nicholas, Vice Captain	England
Laura Davies	England
Elizabeth Esterl	Germany
Sophie Gustafson	Sweden
Carin Koch	Sweden
Catriona Matthew	Scotland
Mhairi McKay	Scotland
Patricia Meunier-Lebouc	France
Janice Moodie	Scotland
Suzann Pettersen	Norway
Ana Belen Sanchez	Spain
Annika Sorenstam	Sweden
Iben Tinning	Denmark

USA	
Patty Sheehan, Captain	Vermont
Jane Geddes, Vice Captain	New York
Heather Bowie	Washington D.C.
Beth Daniel	South Carolina
Laura Diaz	New York
Juli Inkster	California
Rosie Jones	California
Cristie Kerr	Florida
Kelli Kuehne	Texas
Meg Mallon	Massachusetts
Michele Redman	Ohio
Kelly Robbins	Michigan
Angela Stanford	Texas
Wendy Ward	Texas

Photo: David Cannon

Meg Mallon and Rosie Jones

"IT'S A WONDERFUL EXPERIENCE. WE PLAY INDIVIDUAL GOLF OUR ENTIRE LIVES, AND YOU GET SOMETHING LIKE THIS EVERY TWO YEARS. WE GET THE TEAM EXPERIENCE, AND YOU CAN'T DESCRIBE IT UNTIL YOU GO THROUGH IT." Meg Mallon

European exuberance at the moment of victory.

This match was indeed decided there.

In fact, the entire Solheim Cup 2003 was, more or less, decided there.

Most of the spectators attending the second day at Barsebäck have found their way over to the 18th hole.

A beautiful day has turned into evening with the sunset just a few minutes away and there is a stunning view out over the Oresund bay.

Some 10,000 cheering fans stand along the fairway and they can see how Annika Sorenstam, Suzann Pettersen and Laura Diaz place their second shots on the green for birdies.

Diaz, electing to putt first, has the best chance. She is less than five feet from the hole. But, she misses. Now, it's all in the hands of Suzann Pettersen - the 22-year-old Annika Sorenstam of Norway. Pettersen has a putt from 10 feet, slightly downhill. She putts it ... in the hole.

Annika takes a jump of joy. Suzann puts her right hand up in the air before she runs up to Annika and they meet in a huge victory hug. The European fans are wild and crazy, but still civilized.

It's a magic moment.

Annika Sorenstam

Photo: Warren Little

Suzann Pettersen

Photo: David Cannon

Catrin Nilsmark with the victorious Waterford Crystal cup.

Photo: David Cannon

"Playing against the European team in Europe is very, very difficult. They have the 13th man. And when you're in your home country, 13 can be a very lucky number."

USA Captain Patty Sheehan

After the Saturday night triumph Europe "only" needed to win five out of twelve singles matches during the closing day. Europe won eight and the drama was not to be. All the matches are over by 36 minutes past noon and 30,000 spectators still enjoy the sunshine and the splendid show that just ended.

During the three days of competition 99,500 fans have followed the matches live at Barsebäck. Although the majority were patriotic and cheered for Europe, they also were very supportive of the Americans.

"The fans were absolutely fantastic but sometimes it was difficult to know if they applauded us or the USA players," says Captain Catrin Nilsmark.

Her American colleague Patty Sheehan is overwhelmed too: "This is the best Solheim Cup ever and thank you Sweden for this Chamber-of-Commerce-weather."

In his farewell speech, the LPGA Commissioner Ty Votaw says one sentence "thank you for a wonderful week" in Swedish and John A. Solheim, Chairman and CEO of PING, is so impressed that he, during the Closing Ceremonies, personally invites all the 99,500 fans at Barsebäck to the next Solheim Cup at Crooked Stick, Indiana.

The only sad thing about The Solheim Cup 2003 was that it had to end. We, who had the opportunity to spend these three glorious days at Barsebäck, would have loved to see it last for an eternity.

People say that dreams don't come true but this time, they do. Because the next time Europe hosts the event in 2007, The Solheim Cup will visit Sweden again.

And I can't wait.

The winning European team.

Photo: David Cannon

Photo: James Quantz Jr.

2005

Crooked Stick Golf Club

Indiana's best lures Solheim shotmakers

BY PHIL RICHARDS

Photo: James Quantz Jr.

Railroad ties and covered bridges are fixtures on a Pete Dye golf course—the 6th at Crooked Stick.

★ ★ ★

Doc O'Neal's phone rang about midnight. "You need to get out to the golf course," he was told. "It's under water."

Sure enough. O'Neal drove as far as he could. He waded the rest of the way to the clubhouse.

A violent June storm had dumped 2.85 inches of rain on Crooked Stick Golf Club in an hour. High winds had blown over leaderboards, throughboards, everything not anchored, and some things that were. Sixteen trees were down. Another dozen were extensively damaged. Limbs, leaves and litter were scattered everywhere.

There was damage to the main merchandise tent and to the ABC-TV trailer. The hollow in which the 16th green is nestled was a lake; the 7-foot flagstick was submerged, as were parts of the sixth and 14th greens. Bunkers were flooded and the sod wall of the deep pot bunker alongside the third green had collapsed. The canopy on the skybox alongside the 18th green was in the lake. The final round of the 1993 U.S. Women's Open was in jeopardy.

★ ★ ★

Worker removes debris from a water-filled bunker at No. 16 following a 1993 torrential storm that dumped 2.85 inches of rain on the course.

"THIRD TIME DOWN, I FOUND THE PLUG AND PULLED IT." Michael Browning

Photo: The Indianapolis Star

"I picked up some potted plants and set some chairs back up," said O'Neal, a long-time Crooked Stick member who devoted a year to his role as tournament chairman. "I thought to myself, 'Why am I even doing this? It's hopeless.'"

The grate in the creek that drains the back nine and all of Crooked Stick west, through a pipe under the 16th green, was clogged with debris. The only way to drain the area was to locate the plug near the green, and pull it. It was 6 a.m. Michael Browning, a prominent developer and past club president, stripped to his skivvies. He dove in. He dove again. And again.

"Third time down, I found the plug and pulled it," said Browning.

Michael Browning

The water began to recede. Golf course superintendent Chris Hague was everywhere, and by 7 a.m., so was his crew of 35; it had swollen to nearly 200. There was a smattering of volunteers, but the bulk of this militia was members.

They manned rakes and shovels, brooms and pumps. Even buckets. They raked and shoveled and swept and bailed. They picked up sticks and washed greens. Unable to pull the skybox canopy from the lake, they sank it.

By 8 a.m. there was hope. By 9 there was order. The final round would go on, delayed merely an hour, to 9:16.

Judy Bell

"WHEN COMMISSIONER VOTAW CALLED ME AND TOLD ME I WAS GOING TO BE CAPTAIN, I WAS VERY HONORED. TO REPRESENT THE U.S. TEAM AS CAPTAIN IS VERY IMPORTANT TO ME, AND I'M EXCITED TO BE ABLE TO REPRESENT MY COUNTRY AGAIN." USA Captain Nancy Lopez

2005 USA Captain Nancy Lopez

Photo: Courtesy of USGA/J.D. Cuban

Photo: David Cannon

"If you watched on TV," said Browning, "you wouldn't have known anything happened."

Jim Ferriell Jr. knew. The image endures of Crooked Stick's head professional that morning, his jeans muddy, his shirt sweat-soaked.

"Without mentioning any names," said Ferriell, "at one time or another, there were three company presidents and two CEOs fighting over four squeegees." It was Crooked Stick's defining moment, its finest hour.

Ferriell, who now serves in emeritus, still gets emotional over that night and morning. So does Judy Bell, then the U.S. Golf Association's secretary and later its first woman president.

"The heart of the membership is what got me," said Bell. "They have a wonderful golf course, and they are proud of it and should be, but it's the members. I honest to God think they can do anything, that club."

What they will do this September, in partnership with the Solheim family, the Indiana Sports Corporation and the LPGA Tour, is host The 2005 Solheim Cup, and it promises to be historic and hotly contested.

The U.S. team has never lost on American turf. It will seek to regain the Cup, lost two years ago in Malmo, Sweden.

"Passion for Country. Passion for Golf," is the tournament slogan, and it is perhaps embodied by no one so well as Nancy Lopez, who will serve as captain of the U.S. team. Lopez played in the first Solheim Cup, in 1990, and she has some Crooked Stick history, too.

She played here in the 1993 Open, her 17th appearance in the lone premiere event she never won. Lopez was tied for the lead through seven holes of the final round. Everyone on the premises, it seemed, was watching her when she drove into the rough on No. 8. She chopped out, flew a 9-iron approach into the lake and made double-bogey. She shot 74 and finished six strokes behind Lauri Merten.

Little did they know in 1993 when they were paired together in the US Women's Open at Crooked Stick that Pat Bradley, JoAnne Carner and Nancy Lopez would all become Solheim Cup captains.

Photo: Jack Stohlman

"NANCY LOPEZ IS A LEGEND IN WOMEN'S GOLF AND SHE WILL NO DOUBT PROVE TO BE A FORMIDABLE OPPONENT AS THE USA CAPTAIN FOR THE 2005 MATCHES. I FEEL VERY HONORED TO HAVE BEEN ASKED TO BE HER COUNTERPART, AS I DID WITH PATTY SHEEHAN, AND I AM VERY MUCH LOOKING FORWARD TO THE CHALLENGE AHEAD."

European Captain Catrin Nilsmark

Hole # 8: A visible green is difficult to play away from so beware of the left side water carry. The drive must be in the fairway to attack this par 4 hole.

"WHEN YOU PREPARE TO PLAY A TOURNAMENT ON A PETE DYE COURSE YOU KNOW YOU WILL ENCOUNTER EVERY SHOT IN YOUR BAG, PLUS SOME. SOME YOU WILL AGREE WITH...SOME YOU DON'T. THAT'S WHAT MAKES CROOKED STICK A WONDERFUL VENUE FOR THE 2005 SOLHEIM CUP. THERE WILL BE A TIME WHEN YOU WISH YOU HAD A 'CROOKED STICK' IN YOUR BAG." Jane Geddes

Hole # 10: The trouble is on the right side all the way to the back of the green. Direction is more important than length on this par 4 hole.

Photo: James Quantz Jr.

Photo: David Cannon

Jane Geddes

Lopez recalled the bitter disappointment during her first return to the club, in 2004. But already, she was looking ahead. She wants her team to feel the passion.

"I want the players on my team to put their hearts and souls into it, because that's how you win Solheim Cups," said Lopez. "Every player has to feel that way."

The Solheim Cup is, appropriately enough, the international star in a constellation of events. The Big Ten Women's Basketball Tournament was played at Conseco Fieldhouse in March, followed by the NCAA Division I Women's Final Four a few blocks over in the RCA Dome last April. The USA Gymnastics National Championships are at Conseco in August, and The Solheim Cup will have the spotlight a month later, Sept. 9-11.

Enthusiasm is rampant.

Tournament director Kelly Hyne has been involved in five Solheim Cups. When she moved to Indianapolis almost three years ago, she found herself preaching to the choir.

"At other sites, I felt I had to tell the story a lot more," she said. "When I came here and started talking Solheim Cup, everyone knew about it."

Anticipating enthusiastic support for the event, the local organizing committee staged a first-ever random drawing for tickets, which were sold out at 100,000 early in 2005. Volunteers far outnumbered opportunities. The corporate community stepped up.

The Indiana Sports Corporation is a player in big events and this is one it wanted.

"In terms of the kinds of major events we look at, The Solheim Cup scores 9 or 10 in every category," said ISC president Dale Neuburger.

The Sports Corp. brought the 1982 National Sports Festival, the 1987 Pan Am Games and world championships in rowing, gymnastics, diving, basketball, track and field and swimming to Indianapolis. It served as co-host for the 1991, 1997 and 2000 NCAA Final Fours. Its expertise and that of the LPGA, and the involvement of Crooked Stick and the wider community are dedicated, said ISC chairman Earl Goode, to making The 2005 Solheim Cup the best ever.

Crooked Stick completed a course renovation three years ago; its recontoured, regrassed greens are velvet smooth. The club leveled its clubhouse on July 8, 2004 and spent $5.25 million to replace it with a handsome, understated stone structure in harmony with its mission: Golf first, and the first golf of consequence it will serve is The Solheim Cup.

Cup organizers forged a partnership with the Hamilton County Parks & Recreation Department, which will provide Coxhall Gardens for Opening and Closing Ceremonies. The 125-acre farmland property is located across the street from Crooked Stick. Its terraced lawn seating area will accommodate 3,000, and its charms include a waterfall flume, a cascading fountain and 18 acres of placid ponds.

Crooked Stick has been the site of four USGA championships: the 1982 Junior Amateur, the 1983 Senior Amateur, the 1989 Mid-Amateur and the 1993 Women's Open.

Photo: James Quantz Jr.

Hole #15: Your last opportunity for the big wide open drive giving a chance to reach this horseshoe green. Overshooting the front pin, the ball will trickle down the slope while a short shot to the back will fall into the deep bunker.

Considered the "father of modern golf architecture," Pete Dye developed Crooked Stick 41 years ago.

Its first venture into major championship golf was the 1991 PGA Championship. John Daly, the ninth alternate, drove into town at 1:30 the morning of the first round. He was a long-hitting long-shot. He became perhaps the most unexpected champion since Francis Ouimet emerged from the caddie yard at The Country Club to beat British masters Harry Vardon and Ed Ray in the 1913 U.S. Open and club pro Jack Fleck beat Ben Hogan in the same tournament at Olympic Club in 1955.

Crooked Stick was stamped on the public consciousness.

The 1993 Women's Open set records for attendance and corporate sponsorship. The champion's cup went to a self-described "ham-and-egger," a player dubbed "Garbage Queen" by her LPGA Tour peers. Merten exhibited a game considerably more refined than its reputation, particularly on the final day. She played the club's most rigorous stretch, its closing holes, 3-3-3. That's birdie-par-birdie for a 4-under 68 that was one of that soggy day's two sub-70 rounds.

Crooked Stick has been called a lot of things by a lot of people. Pete and Alice Dye call it home. They spend summers in a house on the 18th fairway of the course they consider their "first born."

Pete was a successful insurance salesman and an aspiring golf course architect no one would hire back in 1964. So he put together his own deal. He acquired several hundred acres of land north of Indianapolis, recruited sixty members to throw in $6,000, and over the next several years turned a pool-table flat cornfield into a gently rolling playground of the old world features he had studied at St. Andrews, Muirfield, Carnoustie, Prestwick, Royal Dornoch and 30 other great courses in the British Isles.

Anchoring The Golf Channel telecast of The Solheim Cup from Crooked Stick will be Brian Hammons and Dottie Pepper, while Nancy Lopez (center) will be too busy with her duties as USA Captain.

Hole #1: Only the brave will use a driver on this slightly left to right opening hole. A lofted fairway metal or long iron played to the left side will leave a short shot to the well guarded green.

Alice Dye

"I don't know how in 1964, Alice and I running up and down those hills with no money and no experience, we built green complexes and holes as good as I've ever built," said Pete, 79, and still digging the dirt from beneath his fingernails. "Right to left, left to right, this way, that way, everything balances out, and I know in 1964 and '65, I never gave that a thought. How that evolved, I'll never know."

But Alice does. She smirked. She interjected.

"You just lucked out," she said.

Like Pete, Alice is much decorated. An Indianapolis native, she was the first woman elected to membership in the American Society of Golf Course Architects, and served as the society's first female president. She has won awards and tournaments in bunches, the latter to include the 1978 and '79 U.S. Senior Women's Amateur championships.

Alice will serve as The Solheim Cup's honorary chairman, a position she prizes keenly because she loves the event, and because, "there are no duties."

Crooked Stick is a family club, yet it has no swimming pool, no tennis courts, no tee times and no need of them. With a membership limited to 225, the first tee belongs to whomever chooses to occupy it.

Of the 307 men carried on the club's handicap roster, 162 hold handicap indexes of 10.0 or less. They include club president Dick Beuter (9.4), former U.S. vice president Dan Quayle (6.2), past Western Golf Association president Buffy Mayerstein (4.3), Indianapolis Colts quarterback Peyton Manning (4.0) and Dye (3.0).

Seven women are similarly proficient. They include 78-year-old Alice (8.5) and 1997 U.S. Senior Women's Amateur champion Nancy Fitzgerald (0.0).

Tony Pancake, who succeeded Ferriell as head professional in 2004, teaches six hours a day, six days a week, members only.

"A lot of clubs have members who join to be members of the club, and then they learn to play golf," said Pancake. "Not Crooked Stick. People join this club because they love golf."

It is a happy marriage, The Solheim Cup and Crooked Stick. In a very real sense, the premiere international event in women's golf is coming home, where open arms await.

Photo: Dave Eskridge

Dan Quayle

"I BELIEVE CROOKED STICK IS ONE OF PETE DYE'S BEST GOLF COURSES. THE THREE FINISHING HOLES WILL MAKE FOR GREAT MATCH PLAY DRAMA. NO. 18 IS A FANTASTIC FINISHING HOLE, ESPECIALLY IF A MATCH IS TIED. IT'S HARD TO BIRDIE AND EASY TO BOGEY."

USA Vice President and Crooked Stick member Dan Quayle

2007

Halmstad Golfklubb

Celebrating the community's 700th anniversary

BY TOBIAS BERGMAN

Photo: Courtesy Halmstad Golfklubb

The 12th is the toughest on the back nine, with no bunkers and little room for error.

★ ★ ★

More than a year has passed, but the cheers and applause from the wonderful weekend in Barsebäck, Sweden, are still echoing in Ian Randell's head. The former chief executive of the Ladies European Tour can still feel that sweet taste of victory and revenge, and the corners of his mouth seem to be stuck at that ten-to-two position.

He is in Stockholm to tell the world which course will host The Solheim Cup 2007, and a lot of people at the well-covered press conference in the Swedish capitol think that Randell is just about to press the repeat button.

But he doesn't.

Despite the accomplishment with the course, weather and result in 2003, is Barsebäck not the option to be chosen this time, even if the club would love to have the matches back?

★ ★ ★

"The Solheim Cup 2003 was a huge success and that's also why we wanted to do something different this time. If we had picked Barsebäck again, everybody would have compared the last event to this one and it was hard to make it better. Now we will play on another course and then we have the chance to do that," Randell said.

And the venue which gets the chance to do it is Halmstad Golfklubb, one of the classics among Swedish golf clubs with an impressive track record when it comes to hosting grand tournaments.

The city of Halmstad was born in 1307 when it got its privileges by the Danish Duke Kristoffer. This might seem a bit pointless to tell, but in fact this date played a key role in the campaign for the matches. Because as Halmstad is celebrating its 700th anniversary in 2007, the community wanted The Solheim Cup badly as a major part of the party.

That's also why the community invested a fair amount of money in the bid from Halmstad Golfklubb.

"But it's well worth it. We get the chance to display Halmstad in front of the whole world and that's an opportunity we don't want to miss, especially not now when we're about to celebrate," said Stig-Ove Rick, CEO of the municipal chamber of commerce.

The visitors will meet a city with two completely different faces. Halmstad has always attracted visitors during summer. The atmosphere and spirit of the city and the long-reaching beaches out in Tylösand are two of the reasons. The great golf courses another. In 2000, Svensk Golf, the most widely circulated golf magazine in Europe, stated that Halmstad was the best city for golf in Sweden, and that's probably still the case.

In the evening, visitors invade the restaurants, pubs, clubs and squares which creates a vibrant, almost Mediterranean-like nightlife in the small and charming city centre.

But during winter it's a completely different story with less people, a much lower pulse (and temperature) which probably is needed after the hectic summer season. The Solheim Cup will take place in the autumn, and that means that the city is still alive, though not as overcrowded as during the summer.

Photo: Courtesy City of Halmstad

Modernistic University of Halmstad is one of Sweden's most expansive with more than 7,000 students.

Photo: Courtesy City of Halmstad

The Tylösand beaches guarantee a seaside atmosphere second to none, attracting thousands during Sweden's ideal summers.

"WE GET THE CHANCE TO DISPLAY HALMSTAD IN FRONT OF THE WHOLE WORLD, AND THAT'S AN OPPORTUNITY WE DON'T WANT TO MISS." Stig-Ove Rick

Built in 1938, the long, pine-wooded corridors of the North Course have consistently earned Halmstad Golfklubb its ranking among Europe's top golf courses.

There are many ways of describing the North Course at Halmstad, which is the stage for The Solheim Cup matches. Two words do it better than others: pristine beauty. The holes were carefully laid out in the 30's and 60's by Swedes Rafael Sundblom and Nils Skold, in a forest full of majestic pines. Each hole has its charm, with its own room among the pines. The sometimes quite narrow fairways are lined by the magnificent trees, which also are a great protection for the course. The layout is fair and demanding, fairways and greens are always in good shape but the greatest asset is probably the lack of bad and boring holes. No two holes look the same.

"We're really happy with the way the North Course looks today and we don't need to change anything before The Solheim Cup, though we might do something to make our two finishing holes more challenging," said club director Mats Malmberg.

All famous golf courses have their signature holes; holes where the blood rushes in the veins, the heart beats a couple of extra strokes as the excitement rises. And Halmstad, which is viewed as one of the three top courses on the European mainland, is no exception. This happens mainly on two of the holes. The 12th is a quite long par 4 where a good tee shot is necessary, but the approach is absolutely crucial. It is played from an elevated and sloping fairway over a little but dangerous creek fronting a massive green, where it's important to be close to the flag.

But the best is still yet to come.

Halmstad Golfklubb's 16th hole requires a precision tee shot.

The 16th is voted as the premier golf hole in Sweden, and it's easy to understand why. This lovely little par-3 has almost everything. The tee shot is played from elevated ground to a well guarded green about 175 yards away. Miss right or short means a visit in another little creek; miss left results in a really tough bunker shot towards the green, with the same creek in the background. The always present wind is also trouble on this hole, which surely will be a decisive one in many of The Solheim Cup matches.

The stage is almost set and Halmstad is up for the contest. Last time The Solheim Cup was played in Sweden it was said that it could be Annika Sorenstam's farewell to the event. Then she didn't know that her country was about to host it again. Can she resist the challenge to lead Europe to another victory on home soil?

Don't think so.

"I HAVE GREAT MEMORIES FROM HALMSTAD. I REMEMBER THE COURSE BEING CHALLENGING, IN FANTASTIC SHAPE AND DEFINITELY ONE OF THE BEST WE HAVE IN SWEDEN." Carin Koch

In 2000 Carin Koch's course record 65 at Halmstad Golfklubb
helped secure her first professional win.

Photo: Jerry Rich

2009

Rich Harvest Farms

Rich dreams become reality

BY LEN ZIEHM

Photo: Dale Kirk Photography

Horse paddock and riding areas contribute to the beauty of this pastoral setting at Rich Harvest Farms.

It had always been a dream for Jerry and Betty Rich to own a farm. Little did they know that their love for farm life and passion for golf would some day land them one of the most prestigious women's golf events in the world.

It all goes back to one day when Jerry Rich was about nine years old. Someone had told him he could make some money as a caddie. Rich didn't know exactly what that job entailed, but he was willing to give it a try. His family lived in Wood Dale, Illinois, a suburb west of Chicago, and nearby was Brookwood, a small private club. It was here that Rich would experience his first taste of the sport of golf and would truly get hooked for life.

Jerry and Betty were married in 1961, college sweethearts with a wonderful life and many dreams ahead. After a very successful corporate life, Rich and his wife moved to a small farm in Sugar Grove, Illinois. Mostly a farming town at the time, Sugar Grove was just minutes away from DeKalb, home of their alma mater, Northern Illinois University, but still close to family and friends in Oak Brook.

It was here in Sugar Grove that Jerry and Betty began to develop their labor of love - designing and building a championship golf course as well as establishing a chapter of a successful junior golf program, Hook A Kid On Golf. Their dream and vision of building Rich Harvest Farms and establishing Hook A Kid On Golf will be the Rich's legacy.

The facility began as one hole and a practice area. Inspired by a trip to Augusta, Georgia, and through encouragement by some of Rich's closest friends, including Sam Snead and Bob Murphy, Rich completed the 18 holes of golf in 1998, designing every part of it himself.

After its first year of completion, Rich Harvest Farms was awarded Golf Digest's Best New Private Course in the United States. By 2003-04 it was ranked on the magazine's Top 100 courses in America and was listed as the Chicago District Golf Association's "Toughest Course in the district."

A private country club one hour west of Chicago, Rich Harvest Farms has a small and distinct membership, including many influential men and women. Golfers who are unfamiliar with the facility unknowingly drive through Rich Harvest Farms' enormous main gate into an almost surreal setting, hopefully ready to embark on what will undoubtedly be one of their most challenging rounds of golf.

With a course rating of 78.5 and slope of 152 from the professional tees, Rich Harvest Farms is the toughest course in Illinois. It can be stretched to 7,601 yards when the back tees are used. While challenging, it is not considered tricked-up or overly penal and has the respect of some of the world's top players. Rich Harvest Farms will assuredly challenge the best female players in the world during the 2009 Solheim Cup.

Photo: Dale Kirk Photography

College sweethearts Betty and Jerry Rich had a dream and it became Rich Harvest Farms.

Photo: Hook A Kid On Golf

Hook A Kid On Golf director Holly Alcala instructs Samantha Gates during Chicago Mayor Daley's Holiday Sports Festival.

"JERRY RICH'S MASTERPIECE IS LIKE AN ARTIST CREATING A PAINTING. RICH HARVEST FARMS IS ONE OF THE MOST EXQUISITE GOLF COURSES I HAVE EVER PLAYED." Meg Mallon - LPGA Tour Professional and Rich Harvest Farms Member

An old barn overshadows a Western Junior Championship competitor at No. 2 Silver tee.

Rich Harvest Farms embodies a championship caliber golf course and facilities along with maintaining the natural beauty of a farm-like setting. The golf course is surrounded by endless rows of corn, equipment sheds, horse stables and paddocks which make this place special. Keeping the natural beauty, wildlife and terrain intact was the driving force behind each hole's design. Deer and wildlife are often seen wandering the course or leaving their prints in the dew of the early morning as if to make their presence known. The course itself has several beautiful bridges and winding roads, 400-year-old oak trees and conservation wetlands. During construction, only four hickory trees were cut down. Several natural creeks and ponds made it easy for each hole to develop a challenging and distinct personality.

Rich has always been a man of vision and big dreams, from working in the family business to designing the golf course and several buildings on the grounds including an incredible Plantation House and English Cottage House. The Cottage House is set amongst trees and gives golfers a wonderful feeling as if they are walking down the fairways of Scotland and Ireland. Each house has its own unique characteristics and is elegantly decorated. When you step inside one of the many suites you feel like you are at home. An old horse training area and stable building sits on the west side of the property. Once renovated, Harvest Lodge, as it will be called, will house both the American and European Solheim Cup teams, an amenity few courses could offer.

Walkways and wildflowers abound at Rich Harvest Farms.

Each hole is uniquely named according to some of its special characteristics and features. The signature par-3 hole, 5 Silver, is appropriately titled "Amen Holy Stone." This narrow and challenging green is surrounded by restored and maintained natural prairie grass and wildflowers as well as natural Illinois riverbed limestone. Golfers must be able to get past the amazing view and concentrate on reaching the green.

Another challenging hole is the par-4, 4 Silver, titled "Devil's Elbow." Players must drive in perfect position to hit the green in regulation. This hole has been noted by many as one of America's most demanding driving holes. A full grounds crew keeps the course extremely well manicured, even though the course receives a minimal amount of daily play, only about five to seven rounds. Many have said it could be the best-conditioned course in the country.

During the early years, Rich Harvest Farms was host to a few events. Rich loved sharing his facility with his family, closest friends, amateur golf associations and those who truly love golf. Former high school golf teammate, Roger Ulseth, executive director of the Illinois Junior Golf Association (IJGA) at the time, was one of the first individuals to approach Rich about hosting an annual event. In a joint effort, they created the Illinois Junior Golf Association's annual Roundup at Rich Harvest Farms. This event brings together the top 12 boys and 12 girls in the state of Illinois in a friendly competition now known as The "Rog" in honor of Ulseth, and has been held annually since its inception.

Golfers from Hook A Kid On Golf learn how to drop from a water hazard.

Photo: Holly Alcala

Another local amateur golf association, the Western Golf Association (WGA), uses Rich Harvest Farms as a championship site. In 2003 the WGA held its 86th Western Junior Championship in Sugar Grove. That same year, the members and association were so pleased with the tournament that they awarded Rich Harvest Farms their Centennial Western Junior Championship to be held in 2017. In addition to these prestigious events, Rich Harvest Farms has been a qualifying site for the 2001 U.S. Mid-Amateur, the 2002 U.S. Senior Amateur and the 2003 U.S. Open. The American Junior Golf Association (AJGA) has also held championships there in recent years.

In 1998, a new junior golf association made its home at Rich Harvest Farms. Founded by Rich and lifelong friend, Don Springer, the Hook A Kid On Golf Foundation of Illinois was established as the first chapter of this national program. Under the umbrella of the National Alliance for Youth Sports (NAYS), the Hook A Kid On Golf Program was established in 1990. Its mission is "to provide communities with a comprehensive youth golf program that eliminates the obstacles that discourage youngsters from learning and continuing to play golf, while instilling in them an understanding of golf's rules, etiquette and history."

"RICH HARVEST FARMS WAS DESIGNED TO CHALLENGE THE BEST JUNIORS AND PROFESSIONALS IN THE WORLD BUT ALSO GIVE OUR MEMBERS AND FRIENDS A VERY SPECIAL GOLFING EXPERIENCE."

Jerry Rich

Importance of nutrition captures attention of junior golfers at Illinois Foundation Challenge held annually at Rich Harvest Farms.

"THE 2009 SOLHEIM CUP WILL UNDOUBTEDLY INTRODUCE TO THE WORLD WHAT HOOK A KID ON GOLF AND RICH HARVEST FARMS ARE ALL ABOUT."

Holly Alcala

PGA professional Marc Heidkamp instructs junior golfers at Hook A Kid On Golf outing.

At the time that the Foundation was established, there were 12 program sites throughout Illinois reaching an estimated 420 children. By 2004, the Foundation was managing over 150 program sites, a dozen special events for the kids and communities as well as several charitable fundraisers, including the annual Bob Murphy Pro-Am and Chrysler All-Star Shoot-Out at Rich Harvest Farms. Through the Foundation, more than 150,000 Illinois children have been introduced to golf, its life lessons and the values the sport teaches.

Program Director Holly Alcala, who has been with the Foundation since 1999, leads a talented staff which includes past Hook A Kid On Golf participants who serve as interns. Several different program elements targeting children of different ages and golf ability levels make up the Hook A Kid On Golf curriculum. These program elements are offered to communities and organizations which local Site Coordinators help to plan, oversee and conduct.

Hook A Kid On Golf Foundation of Illinois is also well known for its unique special events. Partnering in 2001 with the LPGA, Hook A Kid On Golf created the first all girls Junior Pro-Am event held in conjunction with the Kellogg-Keebler Classic in Aurora, Illinois. Eighteen Hook A Kid On Golf participants had an opportunity to play alongside LPGA Solheim Cuppers such as Laura Diaz, Michelle McGann and Wendy Ward. The event was held at Stonebridge Country Club from 2001 to 2004 and gave many junior golfers memories that would last a lifetime.

Rebekah Wolf practices during a Hook A Kid On Golf LPGA Girls Golf Club event.

Rich Harvest Farms member Michael Jordan is a big supporter of events benefiting Rich Harvest Farms.

In 2001, a special partnership with the Chicago Public Schools allowed more than 20,000 children in the city of Chicago to experience golf, some for the first time, during a comprehensive golf program established as part of physical education class. Teachers used innovative golf equipment, called SNAG (Starting New At Golf), created by Wally Armstrong, PGA Tour professional, innovative junior golf instructor and friend to Hook A Kid On Golf. This program was so successful that a year later, a national program was modeled after it.

Rich Harvest Farms and Hook A Kid On Golf have been able to provide youngsters with memories and opportunities beyond their imagination. Many of the older Hook A Kid On Golf participants have served as volunteers and standard bearers at events held at Rich Harvest Farms.

The 2009 Solheim Cup will indeed be special for Chicago, Sugar Grove and Rich Harvest Farms. It will provide the Foundation, its kids and communities an opportunity to showcase to the world what Hook A Kid On Golf and Rich Harvest Farms are all about. Keeping in the spirit for which the facility was built, every event that comes to the property benefits the Foundation in some way.

Whether it is the public service announcements or the numerous junior clinics conducted by the nation's top amateurs, indeed, Rich Harvest Farms and Hook A Kid On Golf are synonymous, and look forward to the opportunity to be part of something as special as the 2009 Solheim Cup.

"THE GREATEST JUNIOR AMATEUR BOYS AND GIRLS IN AMERICA COMPARE PLAYING AT RICH HARVEST FARMS TO WHAT IT MUST BE LIKE PLAYING IN A U.S. OPEN." Jerry Rich

At picturesque 7 Gold, a horse trail dissects the hole.

Photo: Jerry Rich

"THE SURROUNDING FARM FIELDS AND NATURAL BEAUTY OF
RICH HARVEST FARMS REMINDS ME OF BEING HOME IN VIRGINIA."

Sam Snead

EPILOGUE

JOHN SOLHEIM
CHAIRMAN & CEO
PING

The LPGA approached Karsten and Louise Solheim with a wonderful idea of an international ladies event between the best women golf professionals in the United States and the best European women golf professionals, similar to the Ryder Cup matches. Though involved in major sponsorship of four events on the LPGA Tour, we looked at this as a great opportunity. The first thing was to work out the details of the agreement between the LPGA, the Ladies European Tour and Karsten/PING. There was going to be a lot of work to do in a short time frame, because the first event was only 10 months away.

We always felt the format of the Ryder Cup worked really well and we were hoping to keep our event very similar. LPGA Commissioner Bill Blue and team had some different ideas on the format of the event, which caused us some difficulties. Fortunately, Joe Flanagan from the Ladies European Tour was in the US attending a Tour event and came to one of the meetings. This was the first time I had met Joe, who had a very solid golf background and was responsible for the negotiations being completed - thank you, Joe. The format of what became The Solheim Cup did end up very similar to that of the Ryder Cup.

One of the early proposals for the name for the event was the Atlantic Cup. After discussions with my parents, Karsten and Louise, I brought back additional suggestions of the PING Cup, the Karsten Cup and The Solheim Cup, being pretty sure which one would be chosen. The goal was to be non-commercial. With our company being named after Karsten (Karsten Manufacturing Corp.) and he being recognized at that time as one of the most powerful individuals in golf by leading sports magazines, they did feel that the Karsten Cup and the PING Cup were too commercial, and all parties seemed pleased with The Solheim Cup.

In our early negotiations, the LPGA suggested having only a few events to get The Solheim Cup started. Karsten, Louise and I broke away from the meeting to talk among ourselves regarding this. We all agreed that we should go with a long-term commitment so there was no question that this would be an ongoing, continuing event. We liked the 10-event (18-year) schedule that my mother suggested with the first right of renewal for future events.

In negotiating this agreement, the LPGA came up with a reasonable figure for the first year. The automatic increases for future years, which were reasonable as well, bothered me at the time as I looked at their future projections. We moved ahead anyway without locking in the future figures. We never did finalize that part of the agreement. Looking back, the original figures would have been a bargain as we approached the long-term projections in only the third event, simply because we wanted the event to be done properly and at a level befitting the finest women players in the world.

We thought it would take some time for The Solheim Cup to mature, since the Ryder Cup had taken quite a while to gain the popularity it has. However, with the Europeans matching the strength and resolve of the Americans as quickly as they did, The Solheim Cup rapidly blossomed into a very competitive tournament. Karsten wanted to be sure the world would see the level of competition we saw in the first two matches so he made sure it was properly televised.

The Solheim Cup also started a wonderful relationship with Waterford Crystal. Kevin Hall showed us some beautiful possibilities and after initial discussions, he came to us with an absolutely phenomenal piece that became The Solheim Cup. I would like to thank Kevin for his contributions to ladies' golf.

Knowing the teams' apparel would be an important item, we strengthened our relationship with Peter Scott of Scotland which already manufactured sweaters for PING. They supplied the sweaters for the teams and staffs for many Solheim Cups and they have been well utilized considering some of the weather conditions that have occurred. Thank you to Rob and Margaret Wight at Peter Scott of Scotland.

I also want to thank Warren and Paul Sunderland of Sunderland of Scotland for providing some excellent rainwear for the teams. Again, due to some severe conditions, they became invaluable to the teams and staffs.

The first few events proved to be precursors for what the competition would be like in the future. The first event was held at beautiful Lake Nona in sunny Florida. Although the score seemed somewhat lopsided, the Europeans consistently hit the ball inside the US team only to see the US team drop the putts. When you have to make the putt, it becomes what this event is all about, having to perform under extreme pressure. During the entire tournament, only the final match on the final day made it to the final hole. The Europeans, however, understood how well they had stood up to the Americans, and had quite a party following the event.

Dalmahoy was the venue that really kicked off The Solheim Cup with the normal (inclement) Scottish weather late in the season. It was great having a facility that could accommodate all the players and staffs for the event right on the site and the golf course proved to be an excellent stage for the second of the matches. The matches here were much closer with seven of eight matches on the first two days going to the 18th hole with the other match settled on 17. The competition was really intense with the Europeans winning on Sunday. It was thrilling just to see the spirit of both teams as well as the intensity of the matches. Both teams played extremely well.

The third event was played at The Greenbrier. What a tremendous facility and golf course this is. Because of the leaves on the trees starting to turn colors at the time of the event, it became even more sensational. Sam Snead, whose house was nearby, stopping by the driving range and talking with us was very much appreciated. Sam and Karsten took time out of the event to participate in the re-opening ceremony of nearby Oakhurst, the oldest golf course in the US. A tradition was begun at The Greenbrier as European and US fans serenaded the players on the first tee.

St. Pierre was a beautiful place with the very friendly Welsh people making us all feel very welcome. This was the only place where the host team did not prevail. To date, this gives the edge to the US in the overall total. This was also the last Solheim Cup that my father was able to attend in person.

Muirfield Village, Jack's course. What can I say about such a great facility. And top that with having Jack and Barbara Nicklaus as hosts… it could not get any better. What they have in place at Muirfield Village to operate an event like this is second to none and helped us and the Tours understand how we could do better with future events. Thank you, Jack. This was the year Dottie Pepper showed how intense passions could be in events like this.

Loch Lomond is one of the premier clubs in the world. Designed by Tom Weiskopf and kept in superb condition under Lyle Anderson's direction, this course proved to be a phenomenal venue for the event. I was truly amazed with the size of the Scottish galleries considering the amount of rain we received. These people love to see great golf competition and they were not disappointed. Thank you Lyle and team for the tremendous condition of the course with so much rain.

Interlachen Golf Club in Minnesota is a world class golf course with quite a history. This was the site of Bobby Jones' US Open victory in 1930, the year he won the Grand Slam. This is also the home of Patty Berg, one of the founding members of the LPGA. All the Interlachen members, their Director of Golf, Jock Olson, and the staff made us feel so at home. This was also the year for the inaugural PING Junior Solheim Cup. Played at Oak Ridge CC, this was an extremely successful addition to the tournament. These players included the current USGA Women's Amateur Champion, the British Women's Amateur Champion and other prominent players in golf. The excitement generated now among young players for playing on these teams is extremely gratifying.

Barsebäck is a wonderful Swedish course outside of Malmo, Sweden. Unfortunately before the event began, Sweden had a terrible tragedy with the assassination of Anna Lindh, Swedish Minister of Foreign Affairs. After hearing what she was like and what she believed in, I know that she would not want her death to have postponed an event like The Solheim Cup, which represents some of the best values her country has. I know she would have been so proud of what Annika and the other Swedish golfers accomplished at the 2003 event. The galleries here were huge and extremely enthusiastic and a new feature was added to the serenading of the players - the members of the junior teams led the cheering for their respective teams. A very special thank you to the Swedish Golf Federation and Gösta Carlsson for the great job they did when we asked for the dates for the 2004 Solheim Cup be moved up to 2003. This was necessitated by the tragedy of September 11, 2001, causing other sports events to be moved. The Solheim Cup will continue to be played in odd numbered years.

Being in Sweden was something special for the Solheim family for several reasons. We had always wanted to have The Solheim Cup played on the European continent and since Karsten was born in Norway, playing it in a Scandinavian country was very meaningful to the family.

Now we look forward to 2005 at Crooked Stick in Carmel, Indiana, another wonderful golf club. PING has fond memories of this Pete Dye course with a young PING tour player (John Daly) winning the 1991 PGA Championship as well as a lady PING player (Lauri Merten) capturing the US Women's Open there in 1993.

In 2007, we will return to Sweden where another great challenge awaits the players. This could be the first time one or more of the previous PING Junior Solheim Cup players makes an appearance on a regular Solheim Cup team. That will really be exciting whenever it happens.

I would like to express my sincere appreciation to Bob Cantin who has taken on the challenges of making sure all the facets for The Solheim Cup meet with our family's expectations in keeping the prestige of this event at the highest level. Much gratitude to John Clark, also, who now performs these services working on the European side.

The Solheim family and all of us at PING are enthusiastic about The Solheim Cups in 2009 and beyond as we will stay involved in what we consider to be the finest event in ladies' golf. We consider it a real privilege to be involved in an event like this where playing for your country and pride is more important than anything else.

We would like to thank the LPGA, LET and all of their staffs and players for allowing us to be a significant part of this extraordinary adventure - The Solheim Cup.

One of my father's greatest joys was having people come up to him and say "Thank you, Karsten!" This was mostly in response to the clubs that he designed and manufactured. In this case, I would like to say "Thank you, Karsten and Louise!" for helping to make The Solheim Cup happen.

The majority of photographs in this book were shot by **DAVID CANNON**. Once a scratch amateur considering a tour professional career, David joined Getty Images News and Sport (formerly ALLSPORT) in 1983 to start the golf library and within three years became a director. His love of golf enabled him to establish Allsport and more recently Getty as the leading source of contemporary golf photographs in the world. David has covered every Solheim Cup event. His award winning golf pictures appear every month in *Golf International*, *Golf World*, *Golf Weekly* and *Golf Monthly* in the UK as well as many other countries around the world.

INDEX

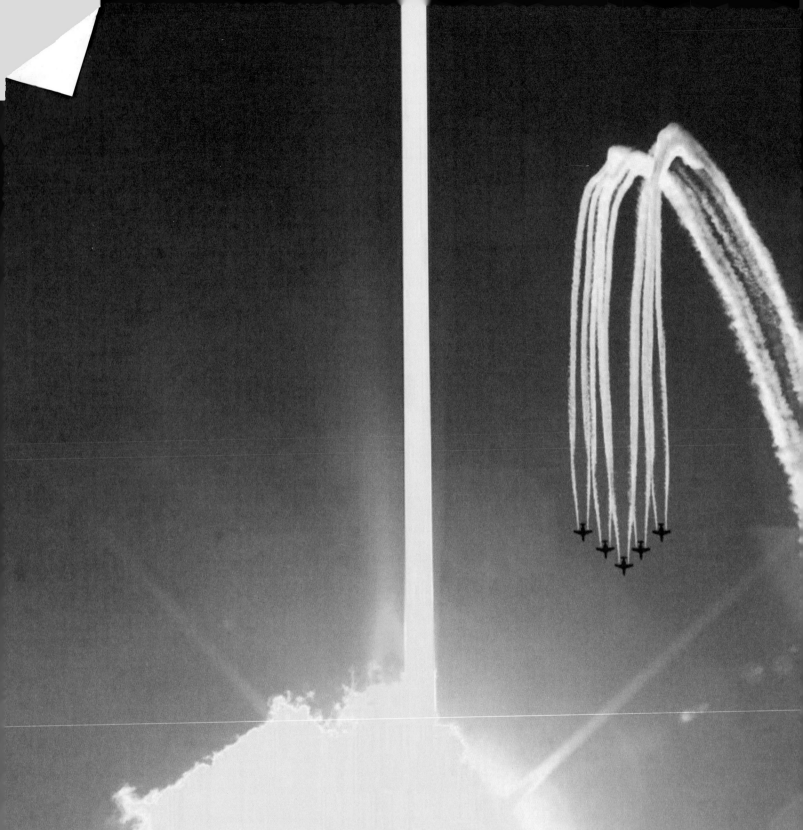

SWEDISH AIR FORCE "TEAM 60"

2003 SOLHEIM CUP OPENING CEREMONIES

Photo: Rick Sharp and Kay Bagwell